# Billy Lane's How To Build Old School Choppers, Bobbers and Customs

# Billy Lane's How To Build Old School Choppers, Bobbers and Customs

*Billy Lane*

MOTORBOOKS

First published in 2005 by Motorbooks, an imprint of MBI Publishing Company, Galtier Plaza, Suite 200, 380 Jackson Street, St. Paul, MN 55101-3885 USA

The information in this book is true and complete to the best of our knowledge. All recommendations are made without any guarantee on the part of the author or Publisher, who also disclaim any liability incurred in connection with the use of this data or specific details.

We recognize, further, that some words, model names, and designations mentioned herein are the property of the trademark holder. We use them for identification purposes only. This is not an official publication.

MBI Publishing Company titles are also available at discounts in bulk quantity for industrial or sales-promotional use. For details write to Special Sales Manager at MBI Publishing Company, Galtier Plaza, Suite 200, 380 Jackson Street, St. Paul, MN 55101-3885 USA

ISBN-13: 978-0-7603-2168-3
ISBN-10: 0-7603- 2168-X

**On the front cover:** Billy Lane aboard Hell's Belle .

**On the back cover:** Billy Lane welding Bobzilla's unfinished fuel tank.

Editors: Darwin Holmstrom, Peter Schletty
Designer: Kou Lor

Printed in China

# CONTENTS

# A NOTE ON USING THIS BOOK

I've been chopping bikes for a long time, and this book represents my best effort to teach you what I know about building bikes. This is not a beginner's guide to chopping bikes. There are other books out there that can teach you that. In this book I want to teach you the detailed techniques I've developed for building unique customized motorcycles—the kind that win televised chopper-building contests and get bikes on the covers of international motorcycle magazines. I'm talking about advanced tecniques here, not how to build a paint-by-numbers cookie-cutter chopper with off-the-shelf parts.

These techniques require you to have a certain level of skill. If you're just bolting together your first chopper, built with catalog parts, you'll want to finish that and get some experience under your belt before trying the techniques in this book. Building a chopper using these techniques will also require some fairly advanced mechanical skills. If you can't pour piss from a boot even if the instructions are written on the heel, I can't help you.

If you aren't comfortable using the techniques in this book, start with a simpler project and work your way up. If you can master the techniques I'm teaching here, you have what it takes to build show-winning customs, so I'll probably be seeing you, and competing against you, at a major show somewhere. Good luck.

# INTRODUCTION
# HISTORY OF THE BOBBER AND THE CHOPPER

By virtue of the design of early Harleys, it was inevitable that they would someday become choppers. These were heavy motorcycles, built more for comfort and long-distance touring than for flat-out performance. Then, as now, the people designing motorcycles at the factory didn't always connect with their customers, so riders were forced to modify their bikes. As with early automobiles, guys found they could make their motorbikes lighter, faster, and easier to work on and maintain if they removed the unnecessary excess. Fenders, exhaust pipes, crash bars, saddlebags, and fork tins were all disposable parts.

Usually, the first things to go were the fenders. Spoke wheels were the only available rolling stock. Inner tube construction wasn't what it is today, and America's roads weren't quite as smooth as those we now enjoy. Flat tires were much more commonplace, and pulling the wheels off an early Harley or Indian to fix a punctured inner tube was (and is) no picnic. For example, the front and rear fenders off my '48 Panhead weigh almost as much as my girlfriend. Removing the fenders from one of these old bikes eliminated considerable weight from a motorcycle that only produced 36 horsepower. Almost all of the early photos of bobbed Harleys I've seen show the bike with no front fender at all. The rear fenders range in variety. Full rear fenders were bobbed by removing the tail-hinge pin and discarding the tail.

Other riders took things a step further, removing the side panels of the fenders just below the stamped reinforcement arch. Some merely unbolted the original fender from the oil tank and frame crossbar, using the fender support as a pivot, and rotated the fender forward. The front of the fender was cut short to accommodate the fender's new orientation on the bike, and the "bob-tail" fender was born. One cool bobber had what looked like a Harley J rear fender attached with a homemade brace.

Whatever the variation, one thing is clear: Bike riders in the 1940s and 1950s were doing what hot rodders were doing. No performance parts were yet available. Prior to the introduction of performance parts, riders used simple and ingenious tricks to enhance performance.

These bikes came to be known as "bobbers": simple, stripped-down hot rods, purposeful, functional, and beautiful. These were the sport bikes—the crotch rockets—of the day, ridden by racers, stunt riders, and badass bikers alike. But as the era wore on, increasingly specialized motorcycles from countries like England, Italy, and Germany, and later from Japan, began to dominate most types of motorcycle racing.

But that didn't stop the owners of American iron from modifying their bikes. Once modifications were no longer aimed at increasing performance, the point became to enhance style. Bikes became longer, lower, leaner; in other words, they became choppers. The "chop" in "chopper" refers to the practice of chopping off parts, a practice carried over from the earlier performance-oriented bobbers, but as often as not riders began adding on a few parts here and there in addition to chopping others off.

Bobbers often featured springer forks from surplus army bikes. These forks were 2 inches longer than the forks on civilian Harleys, which enhanced the ground clearance of the bikes, and thus enhanced off-road performance. The chopper builders took this a step or two (or five or ten) further. Guys like Denver Mullins and Mondo Porras of Denver's Choppers began building springer forks that extended into next week. These forks obviously didn't enhance off-road performance, but they looked wicked cool.

Other aspects of the bobbers became exaggerated on choppers. The combination push bar/fender stay that riders used to push start their dry lake racing bobbers grew and became the mile-high sissy bar that made the back end of a chopper as its outrageous as its extended front end. Exhaust pipes that had been routed high on a bobber to increase ground clearance shot skyward until they looked like a part of a church's pipe organ. If bobbers were about the bare essence of a motorcycle, choppers were all about wretched excess.

Today, people are spending huge amounts of money to buy bikes that recreate these old school bobbers and choppers, which is a good thing if you're in the business I'm in. But you don't have to be rich or have an inside line to a top builder to have your own custom bike. The guys who started this whole thing way back when didn't do it because they had more money than they knew what to do with; they did everything themselves because they couldn't afford to have someone build a bike for them. The original bobber and chopper builders created their custom bikes with tiny budgets, rudimentary tools, and endless resourcefulness. There's no reason you can't do the same. But you'll have something the originals didn't have: me helping you. This book will provide you with all the information you need to build your own old school bobber or chopper.

# CHAPTER ONE
# TOOLS FOR THE BUILD

If you are considering modifying your bike or building one from scratch, chances are you already have an array of hand tools such as screwdrivers, wrenches, pliers, and the like. To chop properly, make sure you have the following basic tools:

- A complete set of ratchets and sockets. Obviously you'll want SAE standard-sized sockets (1/2-inch, 3/4-inch, etc.), but it wouldn't be a bad idea to also make certain you have metric sizes, too (12-millimeter, 14-millimeter, etc.). Most of the fasteners you'll be using will be standard-sized, but should you get a part that uses metric fasteners, you'll be stuck without metric sockets.
- A quality torque wrench. You should have one of these whether you chop or not.
- A complete set of pliers. Again, if you don't already have this, you're in trouble.
- A complete set of open-end and box-end wrenches. Although most parts will use SAE standard fasteners, you'll find an increasing number of metric fasteners on aftermarket parts these days, and sooner or later you're going to need metric wrenches.

- A complete set of Allen wrenches. Like sockets and wrenches, you should have both standard and metric sizes.
- A complete set of screwdrivers, in both flat-blade and Phillips blade styles. This is so basic I shouldn't have to mention it—but how many of you have stripped a screw using the wrong size screwdriver? You need the whole set.
- A complete set of Torx wrenches. These are fairly specialized wrenches. If you ever work on Harley-Davidson motorcycles, you probably already have a set of these. If not, you'll need them.
- An oxyacetylene torch. In addition to cutting metal, this tool is sometimes referred to as a "hot wrench." That's because sometimes when a fastener is hopelessly stuck, a short blast from a torch is the only thing that will get it unstuck.
- Hammers. You'll need a bunch of hammers, like a couple of big-ass mallets for starters, one metal and one rubber. You'll need a ball-peen hammer for more precise bashing than the big-ass mallet. You'll also need a couple of metal hammers with different crowns on their heads, and a couple of plastic hammers. I use a planishing hammer as my primary tool for shaping metal bodywork. These are the brute force tools, and as you become more experienced at old school chopping, you'll grow to appreciate the power of brute force.
- A small grinder. You'll use this for cutting as well as grinding and polishing.
- A variety of manual shears. Having the right cutting equipment can mean the difference between a difficult job that ends up botched and a simple job that is done correctly.
- A hand-held jigsaw. You'll use this on jobs that are too big or too complex for a grinder or manual shears.
- A complete set of files. You probably already have these. If you don't, I don't want to hear about it. Just get them.
- An impact driver. This will help get stuck screws unstuck and should be tried before resorting to the hot wrench.
- An angle grinder. This is a hand-held grinder that you use to cut precise angles. This is critical for cutting parts that perfectly match up with other parts, which in turn keeps your chopper from being as crooked as an Englishman's teeth.
- A wire wheel for your grinder. You'll use this to clean and prepare metal for welding, among other things. This will be especially useful if you are chopping an old bike, because you'll likely need to clean rust off of old parts.
- A motorcycle lift. These are expensive, but you really need one if you are going to work on any kind of motorcycle.
- A hydraulic floor jack. In addition to a lift, you'll often find yourself in need of a tool for lifting heavy parts and holding them in place. These are important, but

I use a planishing hammer for shaping metal bodywork.

should not be used as substitutes for motorcycle lifts, since they don't provide stable enough platforms for working on an entire bike. A 600-pound Harley falling on you will really mess you up.

- An adjustable wrench. These are useful tools, but be careful because they are notorious for stripping bolts.
- Utility knife. If nothing else, you'll use this to open the boxes your parts come in, but you'll find you use it for a lot more than that.
- Electric hand drill. Ideally you'll have a drill press, but even if you don't, you'll find an electric hand drill an essential part of your tool kit no matter what you use the tool kit for.
- Locking pliers. The most common (and best) of these are Vise-Grip brand pliers. You'll find these useful in everyday life as well as in building choppers. They can serve as everything from an impromptu C-clamp to a makeshift shifter, should your bike fall over and break the shifter off.
- A trouble light. Even if you have a brightly lit garage, you'll find the places where you need to work on a bike are shaded from the light. You need a portable light that you can shine on those dark places.
- A pry bar. This is for when you need to multiply the brute force you're applying.
- A comfortable workbench. Not only is squatting down to work on a bike uncomfortable, but it can be dangerous. Squatting in an awkward position for an extended period of time can lead to permanent nerve damage.
- An air compressor. This isn't essential for building a chopper, but it is such a useful tool that you should get one sooner rather than later.
- An English wheel, which is a machine that stretches metal by reducing the thickness of the metal as it passes between the upper and lower wheels under pressure. Again, this isn't absolutely necessary for

building a chopper, but it allows you to create your own metal bodywork so you won't have to use off-the-shelf cookie-cutter parts.
- A small slip roll. This is a machine with three metal cylinders used to form curved metal out of flat sheet metal. These are incredibly handy and relatively inexpensive.

There are a number of other tools you should have to properly work on motorcycles, but many of them are used when doing engine work that is outside the scope of this book, which, as you might guess from the title, involves building your own custom. For this you will need some highly specialized fabricating tools to build and modify motorcycles like a pro.

I began building bikes with virtually nothing, sometimes using my knee as a bending buck. Obviously you won't be able to put my knee in your toolbox, so I'll try to provide a limited guide as to what is fundamentally necessary to create a strong start. You'll have to provide your own knee.

### TIG Welder

The most important and most frequently used pieces of equipment at Choppers, Inc. are our Miller TIG welders. There are three common types of welding processes: TIG, MIG, and Oxyacetylene. Oxyacetylene, often called gas welding, was the earliest and simplest type of welding, but it's still useful in certain applications. This is a lower heat process in which a welding rod is heated by a torch burning an acetylene-and-oxygen mixture. This process is useful when working with thin steel or aluminum. We'll talk about this in greater detail below.

MIG welding, or wire-feed welding, is a bit easier of a process to master, and it's much faster, which is why it's the most common type of welding in mass production. But we're not talking about mass production here. While fast and relatively easy, MIG welding is not as strong or precise

If you do any work at all on motorcycles in your shop, you will appreciate a quality lift.

as TIG welding. In TIG welding a very high heat is confined to a precise point, which melts the base metal to its melting point, allowing fusion to occur. This is by far the most controlled welding process. It allows you to weld strong seams without a lot of metal buildup. After all, what's the point of hand-building a custom bike, if you're going to have a lot of cobby seams that look like they were created by a short-circuited robot?

TIG welding is slow and methodical. At first, using a TIG welder may be precarious, and it's almost always awkward and intimidating, but TIG welding is the way to go for quality motorcycle fabrication. I taught myself to weld with a Miller Econotig. It cost more than I could afford at the time I bought it, but it's been one of my best investments. I have since moved to the larger and more sophisticated Miller

machines, and I truly think they are the best machines I have ever used. I'd recommend buying a book on TIG welding (I highly recommend *Performance Welding Handbook* by Richard Finch, available from Motorbooks) or taking a course at a trade school or community college. This can be a bit expensive and time consuming, but will provide you with valuable skills that you'll be using for the rest of your life. If you want to go the cheap route, take a case of beer to your local welding shop every Friday afternoon and beg to trade for welding lessons. Learning the way I did—teaching yourself—is a slow and grueling process.

If you can't afford a new TIG welder from a quality company like Miller, you might be able to find a deal on a used unit. You can pick up quality equipment from machine shops that are going out of business for a fraction

One of the most important tools in a serious chopper builder's kit is a TIG welder.

the cost of new equipment. Sometimes shops will sell their old equipment when they upgrade to new equipment. Technical colleges are another good source of welders and related equipment. This equipment was made to last for 50 or more years—if you pick up a welder that is 10 years old, you've got a tool that will last you another 40 years.

When you buy a welder, you'll also need a welding helmet. I recommend an electronic helmet, especially for beginners. These helmets automatically darken when you start to weld. This is important, because the hardest part of learning to weld is keeping your torch, stick, or gun aimed properly after you've lowered your welding helmet. The dark glass in a traditional helmet is so dark that you're literally flying blind until the arc starts and you've got a miniature sun lighting up your work area. An electronic helmet can be expensive, but it speeds up that learning curve immensely.

When you start welding, you're going to be confronted by a bewildering array of welding fluxes. Some of them are topnotch; some are total crap. The following is a list of fluxes you will need:

- Number 65 Flux: A good, general-purpose flux that works well on all metals except aluminum and magnesium.
- Solar Flux, Type 1: Works well on nickel and other decorative alloys.
- Solar Flux, Type B: Works well on stainless steel.
- Solar Flux, Type 202: Works well on aluminum.

Whatever you do, don't cheap out on welding rods. If you use cheap welding rods your welds will bubble and boil and leave big, porous holes in your welds.

## Metal Lathes

The second most important piece of equipment in my shop is a South Bend metal lathe. A metal lathe rotates a piece of metal and allows you to shape it. Hundreds of manufacturers produce metal lathes, and they are relatively affordable. I don't know how I ever survived before I owned a lathe. I use mine every day to machine round spacers, cut tapers, and solve the problems other parts manufacturers have built into their "ready to bolt-on" products. The lathe is an invaluable and diverse machine. I prefer the manual variety because it gives me more control, but it also allows a rookie to learn and master the process. One of the first pieces of equipment I bought was a lathe from Smithy Company. One Saturday afternoon I created the first Six-Gun oil cap on my Smithy lathe and turned it into an aftermarket product line that has supported me financially for over 10 years. That is something to think about.

I learned to turn metal on my Smithy with no guidance, but later found a must-have book on lathe operations from South Bend Lathe. The book is called *How to Run a Lathe*. It is small enough to fit in your pocket, but contains more information than a volume of encyclopedias. Buy it, and read it on the toilet instead of *Playboy*.

My Smithy lathe is the second most important piece of equipment in my shop.

## Oxyacetylene Torch

For bending and forming, it is nice to have an oxyacetylene welder or torch. This is basically a pair of tanks, one for oxygen and one for acetylene, with a cutting torch and rosebud tip. A rosebud tip is a multiflamed orifice tip that is probably the most useful of all tips. I use the rosebud to bend my sissybars and top engine mounts, and the cutting torch to cut thick steel plate and metal castings. The oxyacetylene torches are also useful in preheating aluminum for TIG welding and for removing seized bolts and press-fit parts. This is the "hot wrench" I referred to earlier. Oxyacetylene isn't an absolute necessity, but it is so nice to have around, and it's one of the less expensive tools you'll buy, so it would be pretty foolish not to get one. You will use it, and eventually you'll run into a situation where you need it.

**TOOLS FOR THE BUILD**

Another name for the oxyacetylene torch is the "hot wrench."

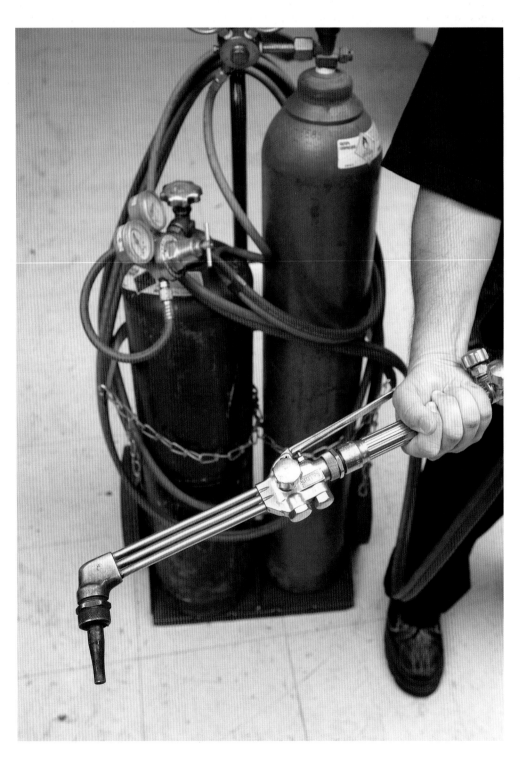

## Milling Machine

Another machine that I was able to get by without for several years, but have become highly dependent on, is my Bridgeport milling machine. A milling machine is a tool that mills material off a solid block of metal, creating the shape a user desires. These are very expensive machines, but if you have one, you can pretty much create any piece of metal you want. If you are going to buy a mill, spend the extra dough and pick up a rotary table. A rotary table rotates to increase the angles from which you can mill material off of a piece of metal. A rotary table will provide a fourth axis to the three a basic milling machine table provides (though some high-end mills allow you to manipulate a piece of metal through five separate planes). The rotary table will allow you to cut radiuses and machine round parts on the mill, whereas only flat parts and linear cutting are generally performed without one. I also use my mill to cope or "fish-mouth" round parts to create a tight fitment for welding operations, and to perform the staggered ball-mill look on the handlebars, frames, and sissybars that Choppers, Inc. has become known for.

As with my lathe, I prefer a manual milling machine over CNC or computer-controlled machines. These mills use computer programs to mill parts from billet metal. Rather than creating the part by hand, the user enters the dimensions of the part into a computer and then the machine mills the metal into the shape of the part specified in the computer program. CNC lathes and mills have become increasingly affordable and have taken over the custom motorcycle scene.

I prefer to do things the old-fashioned way. By mastering my machining skills on manual machines, I have been able to maintain a look in my parts and products that separates them from the majority of the rest of the motorcycle industry. The design approach is entirely different between manual and CNC machines, and that makes a significant difference in the final product.

Once you have a milling machine, you'll wonder how you ever got along without one. I prefer a manual milling machine to a computer controlled one.

**TOOLS FOR THE BUILD**

## Cutting Tools

For cutting flat sheet metal, I use a free standing band saw and a jump-shear when I need to achieve straight lines and square cuts. A hand-held jigsaw can be substituted for the band saw, and I used one for many years before I was able to afford a band saw. When cutting bent sheet metal, I use a pneumatic reciprocating saw or a 7-inch electric angle grinder with a fiber cutting disc. The angle grinder is also great for cutting steel tubing, solid steel bar stock, and pretty much anything else made of metal. I wear out at least one per year.

Plasma cutters are expensive, but they are worth the money.

A day seldom goes by when I don't use my Milwaukee hand-held portable saw.

I also use a Milwaukee hand-held portable band saw on a daily basis. I recently acquired a Miller plasma cutter, but they're expensive. A plasma cutter is an electronic torch that uses very high temperatures to melt metal locally, and a stream of high-pressure gas to cleanly blow away the melted metal. This produces an incredibly clean, even seam, but as I said, a plasma cutter is extremely expensive. I'd recommend spending the money on one of the previously mentioned pieces of artillery instead. A plasma cutter is great, but not a necessity.

## Metal-Forming Tools

I form sheet metal with hand-held metal forming hammers over a leather bag filled with lead shot, and with a pneumatic planishing hammer from Northridge Tools. A planishing hammer is used to produce a smooth surface finish on metal by delivering a rapid succession of blows to the metal. The hammers leave small lumps in the sheet metal, and I flatten and smooth them out with an English wheel from Northridge or a combination planishing hammer/Engligh wheel from Tryrant Manufacturing. The English wheel is a metal shaping tool that produces compound curves in mild steel, aluminum, copper, brass, and some stainless steel.

An English wheel stretches metal by reducing material thickness as it passes between the upper and lower wheels under pressure. This is the same thing that happens when I use a planishing hammer, but it is a lot easier, a lot more precise, and produces a much smoother finish. The lower wheel is called the anvil wheel. They are available with dif-

I use the heavy steel wheel of the English wheel to roll out the bumps the planishing hammer puts in.

ferent crown heights that allow the user to get different contours on the finished part. The pressure between the upper wheel and anvil wheel is controlled by the kick wheel, or hand wheel, located at the bottom of the screw lift assembly under the anvil yoke. This allows you to determine the thickness and hardness of the final part by controlling the amount the metal is stretched.

The English wheel is an ancient tool that has been used to make everything from suits of armor to aircraft parts. And, of course, custom bike parts.

I roll sheet metal, when necessary, in a small slip roll. A slip roll is a machine with three metal cylinders that can be used to form sheet metal into curved shapes. You feed flat sheet metal into the front two cylinders, and the third cylinder in the rear can be positioned to curve metal into any sort of arc you want.

I have some of the other things most of us have in our home garage, like a drill press and a bench vise. You should invest in each of these items. A drill press can be expensive, but it is the only way to drill with the kind of precision needed to fabricate a motorcycle. Bench vises and grinding wheels are less expensive, but no less essential. A bench vise will secure the items you are working on and allow you to work on a part with precision.

I finish the work I fabricate with a 5-inch electric angle grinder with a grinding disc and another with a 5-inch sanding disc. I also use a couple of small pneumatic angle grinders with 2-inch and 3-inch sanding discs when grinding in tight spaces.

I finish fabrication work with a coupe of angle grinders.

# CHAPTER TWO
# PLANNING AND STARTING THE BUILD

I've been building choppers for a living for years, and I have a pretty good idea what I want to do before I start building a bike. I don't have to do a lot of planning before a build, because I know how I want the bike to look. I know what parts I want to put on the bike; I know what existing parts I'm going to use, whether or not those parts are from my inventory or they're something I'm going to have to buy, and what I'm going to have to build myself. But if you haven't chopped a lot of bikes you won't know these things like I do. You're going to have to do some groundwork up front to save yourself a lot of grief down the road.

## What to Build?

First you need to know exactly what kind of bike you want to build. Are you going to build an old-school bobber? Are you going to build a digger-type chopper? Are you going to build an elaborate custom with lots of molded parts? Are you going to use lots of rake or keep the steering geometry relatively stock?

Next you'll need to know the details. What parts are you going to use from an existing bike? What parts are you going to fabricate? What parts are you going to buy? Where are you going to buy them? Are you going to buy an old Harley and chop it, or are you going to start from scratch? If you buy an old bike, how much of it are you going to use in your build? The frame? The engine? Any of the bodywork?

To do this, you need to take an honest look at your capabilities and resources. Chances are you didn't buy all the tools I listed in the last chapter, like an English wheel and a plasma cutter. Without that stuff, you're going to have a hard time fabricating your own tanks and fenders, and you'll likely be buying stuff from aftermarket manufacturers. Pick out the parts you want from reputable companies, then do some research to make certain the parts you choose will all work together. If you buy a frame designed to accept an Evo-style engine and try to install a Panhead engine in its place, you might find you've thrown a lot of money down the drain on either the engine or the frame. But there are a lot of other parts that won't work together, far too many to cover here. Just do the legwork and make certain the parts you choose will all work together. In general, you'll need the following parts:

## Frame

The frame is the skeleton upon which you'll build your bike, and the quality of your build depends on the quality of the frame you use. The frame you choose will determine the look of your bike.

One option is to use a factory Harley frame. You might be building a chopper or bobber from a modern Softail model (the types of frames will be explained below), or you might be chopping an older Knuckle, Pan, or Shovel. If you bought the bike as a complete unit rather than as a collection of parts, you'll have a frame to start with. This might be the least expensive way to go, though it would be best to start with an older hardtail Panhead or Knucklehead if you want to build an old school custom.

If you go with an aftermarket frame, you may or may not want one that has mounting bosses for the tank. Having mounting bosses for the tank will save you a lot of work, but it will lock you in to mounting the tank in a certain spot. Like I said earlier, you need to assess your skills and resources and determine whether you are capable of creating your own mounting bosses. You may want the freedom of locating the tank yourself, or you may need the convenience of having the frame builder locate it for you.

There are several main types of frames, with lots of variations within those types. For example, you can get a traditional hardtail, a raked and stretched hardtail, or a gooseneck hardtail. Listing all the subtypes available would be a book in itself, and a pretty damned boring one, so I'm just going to list the major types. To learn more about types of frames, study the type of bike you like best. Read about the frame used (magazines list this information in a spec sheet that accompanies most feature articles). Once you've narrowed it down, find a chopper builder and start asking some questions. As mentioned above, it doesn't hurt to bring a six pack of your favorite malt beverage when you show up at a shop to start picking some builder's brain.

The following are the major types of frames:

**Hardtail.** This is a traditional frame, with no rear suspension. Depending on the design of the frame, a hardtail features a top downtube that runs more or less from the steering head down to a wishbone that opens up around the rear wheel area. The downtubes then wrap around the axle and head back under the engine area, after which they curve up and head back to the steering head. On some frames, the lower downtubes remain separated all the way back to the steering head, while on others there is another wishbone on the front downtube and only one tube goes back up to the steering head. The advantage of this type of frame is that it gives you a traditional look—this is the type of frame used on motorcycles from the time the first crazy bastard mounted a motor to a bicycle until the late 1950s, when Harley finally joined the modern world and began using rear suspension. The disadvantage is that you have no rear suspension and the ride can be punishing on a rough road. That's the price you pay for a cool-looking chopper.

Though the following paragraphs discusses rear suspensions, I only build bikes with rigid frames. The exception is Michael Lichter's shovelhead pictured in this book, but I only built that because Michael is a personal friend.

**Swinging arm rear suspension.** With this type of frame, the downtubes go below the engine just ahead of the rear wheel area. A swingarm connected to the wheel pivots on the rearmost part of the frame. This is controlled by a shock or pair of shocks attached to the swingarm around the axle area and connected at the top to the frame by a subframe extending back from above the swingarm pivot point. Not a lot of choppers use this type of frame. The most likely way you would end up with this type of frame would be if you started your build with a complete Shovelhead bike. The advantage of this type of frame is that it offers the most suspension travel and thus the best ride. The disadvantage is that it has a modern look that doesn't fit aesthetically with a traditional chopper or bobber look.

**Softail**. Since 1984 Harley's most popular model line has been the Softail series. Softails have the look of an old hardtail, with the frame forming an unbroken line from the steering head to the rear axle, but without the penalty of no rear suspension. That's because a Softail has its rear shocks hidden under the engine. If you are starting your project with a Harley Softail model, this type of frame is obviously the cheapest route. Otherwise, there are a number of aftermarket frames that use this type of suspension. The advantage of this type of frame is that it combines the look of a classic hardtail with a functional suspension. The disadvantage is that while it generally looks like an old hardtail frame, it has too much hardware to really capture the clean look of a hardtail. You can make a good-looking Softail-type custom, but the only way to get the look of a pure bobber or chopper is to use a hardtail frame.

## Wheels and Tires

Tires are a good example of how one decision affects another, and how the choice of a frame affects every other choice you'll make about building a bike. If you want to build a bike with a fat rear tire, you'd better have a frame that will accommodate such a tire. You need to decide how wide your tire is going to be before beginning your build. If you want to use a tire that is a 200 series or wider, you'll need to use an offset kit to move the transmission—and sometimes the engine—over to the left to accommodate the drive chain or belt, or else use a right-side-drive transmission from a company like Baker. That's definitely the way to go if you plan to use a superwide tire, because the bike will be much better balanced if you don't have to offset the engine and transmission.

Most aftermarket frames will allow you to use a wide tire, but if you're using a stock Harley frame you might run into problems. If you're using a stock Softail frame, there are companies that sell swingarm kits for wide tires, but if you're using a hardtail frame from a Pan or Knuckle, or if you're using a traditional dual-shock swingarm frame like those found on Low Riders and Wide Glides, you're options might be more limited.

## Forks

In my opinion many of the modern front ends are visually far too bulky. Some of them are also uneccessarily heavy. I've always preferred springers, though I've built a few bikes with hydraulic forks. Hydraulic forks flex, they're floppy, and I just don't like them that much. Forks come in three basic styles: girder, springer, and hydraulic. Gird-er forks were an older design that used to be common on choppers back in the 1960s, but they are fairly rare today. They consist of a pair of girders with a damping spring in the center up near the steering head. Sprung forks, or "springers," were a later development using a similar concept: two connected fork members with a high-mounted spring providing damping. Hydraulic forks are the most modern of the three designs and use a pair of hydraulically damped shocks to provide suspension damping. This is the most common type of front suspension used on modern motorcycles; they come in either right-side-up or upside-down varieties. The upside-down forks are used on sportbikes and racebikes, and give a bike a performance look, but in reality their benefits are only apparent on a racetrack. On a chopper built for the street, either type works equally well. For that matter, modern springers work pretty well and for all practical purposes are as good on the street as hydraulic forks—at least until the speeds start getting higher than you'll likely reach on a chopper.

Customizing a bike by using a different fork is a long tradition among custom bike builders. After World War II, riders started mounting the springer forks from war surplus bikes because they were 2 inches longer than the factory forks on civilian models. This extra length gave the bikes increased ground clearance, an important consideration in a time when there were a lot fewer paved roads than there are today. Also, people used the same bikes to compete in off-road racing as well as in road racing—there were no specialized dirt bikes back then—so the added ground clearance came in handy.

In the 1960s guys like Denver Mullins and Mondo Porras started building long springer forks for choppers. Denver is gone, but Mondo is still building forks for choppers. You can check out his products at www.denverschoppers.com.

Today a lot of builders are using short, upside-down forks to give their bikes a performance-oriented look. That probably won't look right on an old school chopper or bobber, but if it's what you want, go for it. The point is that you need to decide what type of front end you are going to use before you begin your build, because it will affect your choice of brakes and other chassis components.

## Brakes

Old school drum brakes look great on an old school custom, but they look better than they work. A good disc brake up front and out back will save your bacon more often than you'd ever imagine. There's a wide range of brakes available, most of which are better than the stock parts on even the newest factory Harley-Davidson. This is one component you'll want to spend a little money on. Before you start your build, sit down and make a list of the brake components you want to use, from the brake levers to the master cylinders to the brake lines to the calipers and pads to the discs to the disc carriers and caliper carriers. Then make certain they will work with your choice of handlebar, wheels, axles, and frame.

## Drivetrain

You're going to encounter a mind-numbing variety of engines and transmissions for your bike, from mild, stock factory Harley engines and transmissions to wild, fire-breathing huge-cube chain-snapping aftermarket power-houses with right-drive six-speed transmissions. Again, listing all the options would fill a very large and boring book. The following are the basic types of engines you'll have to choose from:

## Factory Harley Engines

If you are chopping a factory bike, you've already got your engine. And it's one of the following types:

**XL Sportster engines**. These are the "small" twins from Harley, although they can also be the most potent. These range in size from 883-cc to 1,200-cc in stock form. For some reason Harley has always listed the XL engines in metric designations while the Big Twins have been listed by cubic inches. These engines are distinguished by their four-camshaft cases. All four cams are lined up in a row in the right side of the engine case, placing the four pushrod tubes in parallel pairs going up either cylinder. Another distinguishing feature of the XL engine is its unit transmission. That means the engine and transmission are a one-piece unit. The earlier XL engines were made of cast iron, while the later Evolution-type XL engines were made of aluminum. The Evo-type XL engines are much more plentiful than the old Ironhead versions. There is a wide variety of frames and other parts available for XL engines.

**Buell engines**. These are basically breathed-on versions of XL engines used in Buell motorcycles. Their huge advantage is that you can pick up a used Buell for about half the price of a used Harley Sportster. This can be your cheapest source of engine. Prior to Harley's developing the overhead valve Knucklehead, U.S. motorcycle manufactures used a sidevalve design nicknamed the "Flathead." The Indian Flatheads engine are pretty rare in customs these days, but a few Harley Flathead's show up in bobbers.

**Flatheads**. Prior to Harley's developing the overhead valve Knucklehead, U.S. motorcycle manufacturers used a sidevalve design nicknamed the *flathead*. Indian flathead engines are rarely used in customs these days, but a few Harley flatheads still show up in bobbers.

**Knucklehead engines**. This was Harley's Big Twin engine from 1937 until 1947. When introduced, these were high-performance engines, powering bikes that were the fastest things on the road. They still make great chopper engines, but more and more original Knuckle engines are finding homes in pristine restorations. Finding one for a chopper is getting increasingly difficult. Fortunately there are aftermarket reproductions of Knucklehead engines available from several manufacturers. These faux Knuckles can be good choices for your build, provided you buy the engine from a reputable company.

**Panhead engines**. Harley replaced the Knuckle with the Panhead as its top twin-cylinder engine in 1948. The biggest change was the use of aluminum for the head, although the cylinders were still cast iron. Panheads are a bit easier to come by for chopper engines, but again, the easiest way to get a Pan is through the aftermarket, where complete reproduction engines are available.

**Shovelhead engines**. In 1966, Harley replaced the Panhead with the Shovelhead. This engine featured an improved top end, but quality suffered in the 1970s, and a Panhead is likely to be a better choice than a Shovelhead from this period. Quality began to improve again in the 1980s, and the Shovels built between 1981 and 1984 can be good engines for a custom project. If you shop around you can pick up a Shovelhead donor bike fairly cheap, making this a viable option for a chopper or bobber. If you can't find one, the aftermarket can help you out; S&S now offers a complete reproduction Shovelhead engine.

**Evolution engines**. In 1984 Harley replaced the aging Shovelhead engine with the all-aluminum Evolution. This is the engine that powered Harley back from the brink of extinction. Most aftermarket engines are of the Evolution type. The price of used Evos is coming down, too, meaning it's possible to pick up a factory donor bike at a reasonable price.

**Twin Cam engines**. The Twin Cam replaced the Evo in 1999 and 2000, about the time that Harley ramped up production well past the 200,000-bike-per-year mark. That means there are probably more Twin Cams on the road than any other factory Harley engine. But because these bikes are fairly new, finding one cheap enough to use as the basis for building a chopper or bobber could prove a problem. At the time of this writing, S&S marketed a complete Twin Cam aftermarket engine, but Harley had sued for copyright infringement. How that works out remains to be seen. The Twin Cam is a definite improvement over the Evolution, providing better oiling and a stronger bottom end.

There is no right or wrong engine. Obviously a traditional engine like a Pan or a Knuckle or even a Shovel would look more correct in an old school chopper or bobber, but it's your bike and your decision. The important thing is that you pick a frame-drivetrain combination that works well together.

## Transmission

Choosing a transmission can be as bewildering as choosing the rest of the cycle parts to use on your custom bike. You'll have a choice of four-, five-, and six-speed transmissions in either right or left drive configurations. That is, the drive sprocket shaft comes out of the right- or left-side of the transmission. Obviously this dictates that the drive belt or drive chain is on the same side of the bike as the drive sprocket.

Stock Big Twin Harleys—Knuckleheads, Panheads, Shovelheads, Evolutions, and Twin Cams—have the final drive assembly (chains and sprockets or belts and pulleys) on the left side of the bike (when you're standing beside the bike facing the front of the bike). Sportsters have always had the final drive assemblies on the right side of the bike. The XL engines in Sportsters use unit construction; that is, their engines and transmissions are built as a single piece, so it would be difficult to use a complete aftermarket transmission in such a bike. But Big Twins have separate engines and transmissions, so mounting an aftermarket unit is generally as easy or difficult as mounting a factory unit.

Many modern customs use a right-side-drive transmission because it allows the use of a wider rear tire without having to use too much driveline offset (see the next chapter). Since we are building old school customs here, and since the most traditional engine for an old school custom is a Harley Big Twin, which has always used left-drive transmissions, we'll only discuss the use of left-drive transmissions. The most important thing you need to know about using right-drive transmissions is that their use dictates using a variety of other parts to match, like wheels, brakes, brake carriers, axles, spacers . . . the list goes on and on. Like everything else when building a custom bike, your choices in one area affects every other area of the build.

## Belts or Chains?

Another drivetrain question you need to answer before starting your build is whether you want to use a chain or belt primary drive and a chain or belt final drive.

A chain final drive will allow you more options for gearing the bike than will a belt. That's because there are more choices for chain sprockets than for belt pulleys. The size of your sprockets is part of your bike's final drive ratio, just like the size of the gears in the rear end of your car is part of your car's final drive ratio. If you increase the diameter of your rear sprocket pulley or decrease the diameter of your front sprocket or pulley you'll lower the final drive ratio of the bike. This will increase acceleration off the line at the expense of top end performance. If you go the opposite route and put a smaller sprocket or pulley on the back or put a larger sprocket or pulley on the front, you'll have a bike that turns lower rpm on the highway at the expense of decreased acceleration off the line. If you don't already know what you want, find a helpful mechanic and ask for his or her advice. As always, a refreshing beverage can help loosen the mechanic's tongue.

Except for a few limited production models from the early 1980s, most stock Harleys use a chain primary drive. These are reliable and relatively low maintenance, and if you're building your chopper or bobber from a stock bike, you've already got one. Belt primaries are lighter and look cooler, but they are expensive to buy and can mess you up pretty good if you get your pant leg caught in one, since most aftermarket belt primaries run out in the open. Another good example of how one choice affects another choice is that if you run a belt primary, you'll need to use a dry clutch. Some stock Harleys have wet clutches—the clutches run in an oil bath—and some have dry clutches. If you've got a bike with a wet clutch and want to run a belt primary, you'll need to invest in a dry clutch.

# CHAPTER THREE
## DRIVELINE SETUP

Do the hard stuff sober when building your bike. Save the partying for after you're done working.

Every time I build a custom motorcycle, I begin work at the rear of the bike.

## Centering the Rear Wheel

The obvious first step in building, from my perspective, is centering the rear wheel and tire in the frame you plan to use. The best way to do this is to slide the axle through the frame and rear wheel, and visually center the wheel. Take a rough measurement of the exposed axle on each side of the wheel's hub, between the frame's axle plates. Install axle spacers on each side of the hub to cover the length of exposed axle on each side. Some people use PVC pipe, some use washers from the hardware store, some use axle spacers from God-knows-where. I machine my spacers on my lathe from 1.5-inch-diameter aluminum bar stock, but I've tried every method mentioned and more. Whatever works is good enough. The key is to locate that rear wheel in the frame somewhere close to the frame's centerline.

When I think I am close, I measure. I have a reputation for not measuring, but when my ass is on the line, the rulers appear. Do this sober, because it can and will come back to haunt you if you mess it up. This is technical. Save the high for the artistic chapters.

I center the rear wheel using the frame's backbone as my centerline. By placing a straight edge on either side of my rear wheel and measuring the distance from each straight edge to the backbone, I am able to determine how far off from reality my eyesight is.

One of the best straightedges I have ever found is a tubular fluorescent light bulb. If you pull one out of the garage ceiling, things might get dark for you, so wait until the wife isn't looking, and rob one from the kitchen. She'll understand after you take her for her first ride.

Properly centering the wheel in the frame requires measurement.

I place a straightedge across the surface of the sprocket to ensure that the drive chain will clear the rear tire.

The distance from each straightedge to the backbone should be the same. By manipulating the axle spacer length on both sides, I am able to obtain equal measurements and center my rear wheel. I machine my spacers in a lathe in order to find this balance, and move forward.

## Driveline Alignment

With the advent of wider-than-stock tires, aligning the driveline has become an absolute necessity. The wider tires require that the rear drive chain or belt be moved outward from its original location in order to pass the tire without making contact with it. The distance the rear drive is moved from its original location is called the final drive offset or secondary drive offset.

When I use a typical wide 240-millimeter Metzeler tire on an 8.5-inch rim, I move the final drive outward from center by roughly 2.5 inches. Realize that I am using the term "center" not as a reference for measurement in this case, but for direction. In other words, I move the final drive toward the left side of the bike 2.5 inches further than it is originally located from the frame's centerline. The magic number isn't always 2.5 for that tire and rim combination, but it is a nice even number that I can aim for. Some frames and drive-side brake systems may make it impossible to move the final drive out this far. Which brings us back to my point: I work from the rear forward. Sometimes I have to come back and adjust my final drive offset. More on that later.

Once I am confident that I have achieved final drive alignment, I clamp the transmission plate to the forward transmission mount and weld the rear mounts in place.

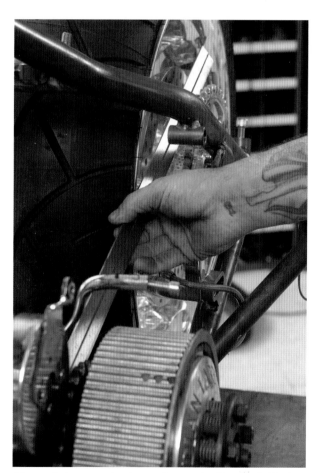

**Above:** I always recheck my alignment with a straightedge after I have completed my welding. A mistake here can cost me big time later.

**Left:** With the transmission set loosely in the frame, I align the inside edges of the transmission sprocket and the rear wheel sprocket using a straightedge.

I need to install the engine in the frame to determine the primary-drive offset. This offset is different from bike to bike, and it is the most difficult to determine properly. The rear wheel, transmission, and engine must all be securely bolted in place to achieve success.

A Rivera belt drive primary pulley with offset Evo insert.

*Bobzilla's* engine is a Knucklehead with a tapered sprocket shaft. I have to fabricate the offset primary pulley insert required to give me proper alignment. I begin by using two pulley inserts from Rivera Engineering. By combining a standard insert for the tapered shaft (pictured on the engine's shaft) with an offset insert for an Evo engine (pictured inserted in the pulley), I am able to machine and weld together the necessary part.

By taking measurements from my straightedge reference, I determine how much material needs to be machined from the Evo pulley insert to give me the proper alignment between the two primary pulleys.

With the Evo pulley insert chucked squarely in the lathe, I need to perform two operations: face it to the correct length and counterbore the splined center for the Knucklehead insert.

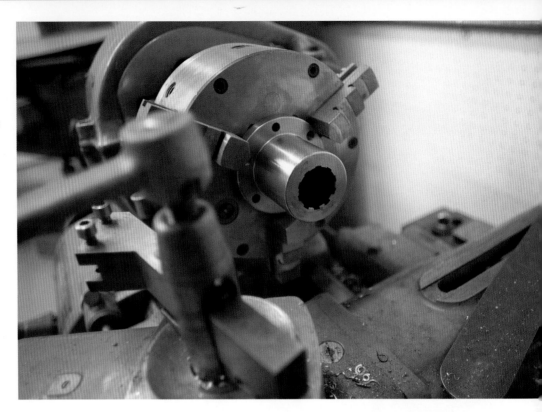

This is the facing operation. Note the black line I made on the insert with a Sharpie. This mark lets me know visually when I am getting close to my correct length.

This is the counterboring operation. I perform this cut by removing the compound rest from my lathe and installing the boring bar attachment and boring bar. I counterbore the Evo pulley insert so that the Knuck insert will make a press-fit into the bore.

Here I have the Knuck insert pressed onto the tapered shaft. I will tap the two inserts together using a brass mallet.

A detail view of the pressed-together inserts installed on the shaft. I always rotate the engine and check for runout before welding these two parts together.

Another thing I always do before welding the pulley inserts together is install the primary belt and front pulley for a visual check.

**Above:** This photo illustrates that I measured improperly somewhere. Notice that the outer edge of the front pulley doesn't align properly with the belt. I am going to have to go back to the lathe and remove some more material from one of the inserts. It is a good thing I didn't weld the two together yet.

**Left:** I use a straightedge and dial caliper to determine exactly how much material I need to remove from the front pulley insert.

After I machine a few more thousandths off the insert, my straightedge tells me that I have proper primary driveline alignment.

Nobody makes a sprocket-shaft nut that fits inside the custom pulley insert I fabricated, so I will have to make one from two sprocket-shaft nuts. This is accomplished by machining a counterbore in one nut, and turning the end of the other down to make a press-fit inside that counterbore.

This photo shows the two machined nuts pressed together and fixed in vise jaws.

I TIG weld the nut in the vise. I have to add tremendous heat to fuse the two pieces together with adequate penetration. This is a part that nobody wants to see come unglued. I'll turn the welds down in the lathe when the welding operation is completed and cooled, so that there are no high spots at or near my welds.

This is what the welded and completed pulley insert and nut look like.

With all of the machining and welding heat that I have introduced to these parts, it is a good measure to install them both on the sprocket shaft and check runout one more time. When I am happy with the results of that check, I can move on to the final steps of checking, and achieve my driveline alignment.

I always like to crank the sprocket-shaft nut down hard with my impact gun. If that press-fit and weld are going to give, I want to know in the shop and not on the side of the road.

A final check making sure everything is in order. Here, I move the transmission back to tension the primary belt and torque the transmission mounts.

## Final Drive Offset

The first and most important factor in a properly aligned driveline is the final drive offset. Final drive offset may be achieved in three ways. The first way is by force. Some custom wheels, especially billet wheels, come with a hub machined wider than stock on the drive side. This wider hub is meant to provide built-in final drive offset. I never trust anybody, so I don't believe in simply bolting my drive sprocket or pulley to anyone's hub and hanging it in the frame. I always check visually to see that my final drive will clear the tire. Sometimes I find that the wheel manufacturer has made the hub too wide. Falling for a manufacturer's false claims is a huge mistake, and one that depends on your own stupidity and complicity to be successful. Don't fall for it. More often than not, I machine a brand new hub down to where I want it. Where I want it is where it really needs to be. Remember, most aftermarket custom parts are made to suit the masses. If you fall for their tricks, your custom bike will look and feel like those owned by the masses. And that means it will look, run, and ride like shit, if it runs and rides at all.

The second way to create final drive offset is to place a spacer between the wheel hub and the drive sprocket or spacer. Drive spacers in a variety of thicknesses may be purchased pretty much anywhere you find custom parts. On occasion, a spacer may need to be machined a few thousandths to achieve driveline alignment. However, we try to avoid doing this as it is both costly and what is known in the business as *a pain in the ass.*

The third way to produce a final drive offset applies only to laced or spoke wheels. I don't recommend it (though I've done it many times myself). This method requires releasing the tension on all of the wheel's spokes, and moving the hub toward the drive side of the wheel by means of tightening only the spokes on the left side of the wheel. I then tighten the spokes on the right side of the wheel. I have been able to relocate the hub 3/4 inch this way, but it disrupts the spokes' natural angular relationship. My dad always said "any port in a storm." This is the "any port in a storm" solution to the offset situation.

## Transmission Offset

Assuming that the final drive offset is where I want it, the next step in setting up my driveline is determining the transmission offset. This term refers to the distance that the transmission is moved outward from center. Transmission offset is dictated by several factors, each crucial to a properly aligned driveline.

Naturally, the final drive sprocket or pulley on the rear wheel must align correctly with the drive sprocket or pulley on the transmission's output shaft. Therefore, the final drive offset described above will roughly dictate the transmission offset. One would think that if the rear drive sprocket is moved out 2.5 inches, then the transmission would need to be offset 2.5 inches to find correct

alignment. If everything were standardized, that would be an accurate assessment. What makes determining this particular offset difficult, though, is the variety and combinations of transmissions, main drive gear spacers, and sprocket and pulley offsets that have to be factored into the equation.

The best way to eliminate these variables is to throw the rule book into the garbage with the empty beer cans. Instead of using mathematics and measuring, I rely on true alignment. I place a straightedge ruler across the outer surface of the rear drive sprocket or pulley and move the transmission outward until the outer face of the transmission drive sprocket or pulley touches it. This is when you know you have met your goal. The transmission plate holes may not match the holes on your frame, but this doesn't really matter. I never bolt my transmission plates to the frame until I am sure the entire driveline is true. There is no need to measure how "far off" the transmission is from its original expected location. The important thing to know at this point is that two of the three driveline components jibe.

If the transmission plate doesn't seem to line up with the frame, there are remedies. One is to machine the holes in the transmission plate into slots, which will allow for the alignment of the plate with the frame. Another is to find the transmission plate's natural resting point, as dictated by the final drive offset, and weld the transmission plate to the frame. I know welding seems very permanent, like marriage, but how many times do you plan on building this bike? If you do it right, once is enough . . . in both instances.

## Determining Primary Drive Offset

The third of four steps in setting up the driveline is determining primary drive offset. The engine must be securely bolted in the frame to measure this distance. Primary drive offset is the distance between the primary drive's present location (due to the final drive offset and its relationship with the transmission offset) and the location of the engine. Measuring this offset isn't an option. It has to be determined empirically. I find this distance by mounting my clutch hub and basket securely to the transmission mainshaft. Since I know my final drive offset is, say, 2.5 inches, I slide a primary drive pulley with a 2.5-inch insert onto the engine's output shaft. Placing a straight edge across the outer surfaces of the clutch basket and engine drive pulley, I am able to determine whether I am correct, in the ballpark, or screwed.

Using a vernier caliper, I am able to determine the primary drive offset. The solution to correcting this offset is to use an offset insert between the engine and the front primary pulley. For example, if I determine my primary drive offset to be 1.25 inches, I would use a 1.25-inch primary pulley offset insert. And if my primary drive offset is determined to be 1.30 inches, I would use a 1.50-inch insert. However, in this instance, I would need to machine 0.20 inches off the insert in order to achieve my desired offset of 1.30 inches.

## Setting the Driveline Length

All of this alignment brings us to the fourth and final determinant in driveline setup—setting the driveline length. Driveline length is primarily dictated by the primary belt or chain length. Aftermarket primary belt drives, and stock and aftermarket primary chain housings, usually predetermine the primary drive length. You simply bolt the inner primary housing or billet plate to the engine, slide the transmission forward or backward so that its bolt holes align with those belonging to the primary, and secure the transmission to both the primary and the transmission plate. However, some open belt primary drives feature adjustable backing plates, and early four-speed belt and chain drives didn't enjoy the strength or determining service of any backing plate at all. In these instances, the best way to set the primary drive length is to slide the transmission back to tighten the primary drive belt or chain. There has to be a little slack in both for the clutch to be able to work properly for any extended period of time.

## Rear Drive Tension

Once the transmission is tightened down securely, the only thing left to do is to create the correct tension in the rear drive by moving the rear axle backward in the frame. This final drive length may be manipulated in several manners:

1. Adding or removing chain links, if you are running a chain.
2. Changing pulley or sprocket diameters.
3. Changing rear belt lengths.

For riders of shorter stature, it is sometimes better to run the rear wheel as far forward as possible to bring them closer to the handlebars. Using one or more of the methods described may help achieve this end.

## Engine Top Mounts

Only after the driveline setup is completed is it practical to build a top engine mount. I can't remember how many times I've had a friend or customer complain to me that their bike mysteriously began running poorly or became completely and hopelessly untunable. Nine times out of ten I have been able to solve or eliminate the problem by retightening all seven of the engine mount bolts. The three top engine mount bolts are most commonly the weak link in the chain, due to the vibratory energy and reciprocating mass within the Big Twin engine. Because of that, I consider a solid and well-built top mount to be absolutely crucial to the enjoyment of riding any chopper. If the top mount is weak, the vibrations of the engine will make their way uncontrollably through the rest of the bike. This is how frames, gas tanks, and mounts break, and how what doesn't break rattles off and falls onto the highway.

I don't ever buy top engine mounts. I make every one specifically for the engine and frame to which it will belong. I use counterbored and drilled 1-inch-diameter round steel stock at each cylinder head bolt hole and at the frame's top bolt hole. Choppers, Inc. makes a custom builder's kit that includes these pieces. The kits save considerable fabrication time and money. Between the three round pieces of steel stock, I use cut lengths of 3/4-inch-diameter cold-rolled steel round stock to form the frame of the top engine mount.

The angles at the ends of the bar stock are always complex and never the same, so I cut the end of the bar stock with a cutting wheel and grind fish-mouths into the ends on the grinding wheel instead of coping them in the milling machine with an end mill. Sometimes it takes several attempts to get the fitment right, but it is an extremely quick method in comparison to the alternative machine shop setup. When everything fits well, I TIG weld the top mount frame pieces to the three pieces of round stock. I always create a deep, penetrating, bonding puddle with the TIG torch, then fill and cool the puddle with a 1/16-inch mild steel filler rod. Top engine mounts don't come stronger than this. They are a small but critical piece of the chopper puzzle.

CHAPTER FOUR
# CHASSIS CONFIGURATION AND MODIFICATIONS

At Choppers, Inc., I only build choppers and bobbers with rigid frames. The one exception is the four-speed swingarm-framed bobber I am doing for the famous photographer for *Easyrider* magazine and my first book, Michael Lichter. I typically build bobbers with stock frames, 30 degrees of neck rake, and no frame tube stretch. My choppers are usually raked at 45 degrees with 4 inches of frame backbone stretch and 6 inches of frame front-leg stretch, or raked at 50 degrees with 4 inches of backbone stretch and 8 inches of frame front-leg stretch.

I like to use stock Knucklehead handlebars, or my custom TittyBars on my bikes. I make a TittyBar Builder's Kit. The Builder's Kits allow anyone with a welder to assemble the bars themselves, and configure them so they fit the look and feel of the buyer's own bike. The kits come with an internal throttle. Here, I weld the throttle sleeve into the right bar section.

This is the left side bar section. Note the plug welds that hold the outer sleeve to the inner sleeve. The inner sleeve is 1-inch-diameter frame tubing to accommodate standard hand controls.

The internal throttle inner sleeve plug welded to the 1-inch tube.

I tap the throttle part into the outer tube with a brass mallet.

I have to check the length of the bar assembly, then plug weld it so that it is sturdy.

This is just one example of a finished set of TittyBars I made from a Builder's Kit.

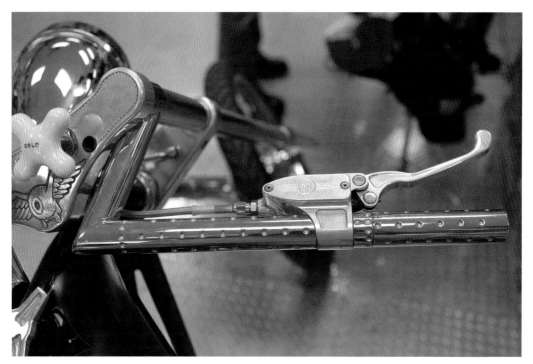

This detail of the right side handlebar shows how nicely the bars accommodate the Performance-Machine Contour master cylinder. It also shows how seamlessly the throttle fits the bars.

## Suspension

I prefer to run a stock-length springer fork, Indian-type leaf-spring springer fork, or Hydra-Glide hydraulic fork on the bobbers. With the first chopper frame I described, 12 inches of extension works well, and 16 inches of extension sets the second up just right. I prefer springer forks on the choppers, because the way springer fork rockers kick the wheel out in front of the fork generally overcomes many of the performance and handling problems associated with poor rake and trail combinations. Springers tend to be bouncy and experience more flex than hydraulic forks, but they have and build character.

## Brakes

Front brakes may be a valuable asset in sticky situations, but I leave them off of my personal bikes. I like not having a front brake, even though they have no doubt saved my life on more than one occasion. I prefer the clean handlebars and open wheel look the absence of a front brake provides. Riding without a front brake has definitely made me a more cautious—and sometimes more aggressive—rider. However, I have built many bikes for my customers, and a few for myself, with a front brake. Performance Machine and Jay Brake, in my opinion, manufacture the best disc brake components in the aftermarket industry.

I love a mechanical drum rear brake on all of my traditional style bobbers. The best looking and best performing rear disc brake configuration I have tried on my choppers is the inboard brake setup, where the disc brake rotor is located inboard of the rear belt drive pulley or rear chain drive sprocket. I like to run a four-piston Performance Machine billet caliper over an 11-inch floating brake rotor in this situation, with a P-M 5/8-inch-bore master cylinder.

On *Bobzilla*, I used a Performance-Machine inboard brake system. With the wheel centered, I place the caliper over the rotor in order to determine where to place the caliper mounts.

I cut sheetmetal strips and slip them between the brake pads and the rotor on both sides. This method ensures that the caliper is square to the rotor's surface, and it holds the caliper in place while I fabricate the mounts.

Performance-Machine's caliper mounting bracket interfered with the axle plates on *Bobzilla's* frame, so I removed the tail end of it with a cutting wheel. I'll go back later to machine the cut surface smooth and repolish the bracket.

After bolting the Performance-Machine mounting tabs to the bracket I modified, it is clear that I am going to need to fabricate some extra pieces to bridge the gap between the frame and the supplied tabs.

Using part of a manila office folder, we make a template for the metal bridge. The template will be transferred to a piece of steel, which I will cut to blend nicely with Performance-Machine's tabs.

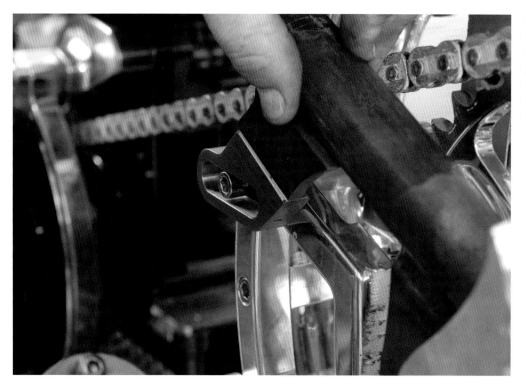

I check the fitment of the steel bridge prior to welding. It is important to fabricate the part with a tight fit—the end result is at stake.

With everything snug, I TIG weld the bridge to the frame and the tabs to the bridge.

A nice, even, penetrating weld is critical to keeping the rear brake bracket in place. My ass is riding on these welds . . . literally.

Performing a fish-mouth or coping operation in the milling machine with a hole cutter.

CHASSIS CONFIGURATION AND MODIFICATIONS

After the coping operation, the tube is ready to be fit to the frame tubing. The coping cut eliminates the need for gap welding.

With the bracket welded where we want it, the open end needs to be cut to an angle that will let the tag rest squarely with the bike.

Prior to welding the tag mount tube to the frame, I mark the spot on the frame with a Sharpie where I want to place the tube. I drill and bore a hole at my mark, through which the tag light electrical wires will pass.

Ken welds the tag bracket in place.

Ken bolts the tag backing plate to one of the tag mounts that is included with the Choppers, Inc. Builder's Kit. Using the backing plate during this step allows Ken to watch the welds pull as they cool. The cooling welds will pull the backing plate crooked. Ken is able to visually adjust the backing plate as he finishes the welds.

Notice how tightly the tag bracket pulls the tag into the frame. It needs to be visible, but I don't want it hanging out so far that it is in the way of everything.

## Riding in Comfort

One of the most misunderstood facts about choppers is that they are not very comfortable to ride. This is a huge misconception, and I am here to clear it up. Of course, a full bagger with armrests and a lumbar support is more practical for cruising North America than one of my rigid frame choppers. However, that is not to say that a chopper or bobber can't be ridden on extended trips with moderate comfort. I have made the trip to Sturgis from Florida on several of my custom choppers, riding up to 725 miles in one day.

The key to making a chopper or bobber comfortable is posture and rider positioning on the bike. What I like about rigids is that the rear fender meets the frame in a way that provides a natural cradle, which lends itself to excellent hip positioning. Rider hip position is highly important to lower back comfort. A low cradle-shaped seat on a rigid bike sets the rider back and down in the bike, where the high, flattened-out seat on a Fatboy places the rider up, forward, and over the bike.

Handlebars are another sore subject when comfort is mentioned. I used to run apehangers, but too many stops on the side of the road by law enforcement put an end to that. I switched from the apes to drag bars, and eventually developed two of my own versions of drag bars. One version is called WhiskeyBars, which got their name one morning when I walked into the shop with a heavy whiskey hangover and noticed a pair of handlebars on my Shovelhead that I still do not remember ever making. They are basic drag bars with a miter cut, welded together in the middle. The mitered cut can be varied, allowing for different amounts of pullback. The second version of drag bars I like are called PrisonBars, which were created for my friend George, whose bike I was building at the time of his release from prison. WhiskeyBars and PrisonBars are virtually the same, except that the WhiskeyBars have bends in them between the center weld and each end, and the PrisonBars are straight.

I later developed a style of making handlebars out of 1 1/4-inch ball-milled frame tubing, and named them Titty-Bars. The name doesn't have any significance other than that I have spent a lot of time in strip clubs and I guess they've rubbed off on me (pardon the pun). TittyBars have 1-inch frame tube sleeves inside the larger tubing and contoured reliefs to accommodate Performance Machine's Contour Series handlebar controls. They also have an internal throttle.

Handlebars have become a big part of the style of my bikes. On bobbers, I love the original style H-D springer speedway style bars. On my choppers, I prefer the TittyBars run as low as possible to the forks. Sometimes I even mount the TittyBars below the top fork tree and bring them up and out. My style was heavily influenced by the clip-on race style, running the bars below the top of the fuel tank long before it was cool on the street. I don't think that look will ever not be cool. Racing will be here long after you and I are gone, and it'll no doubt continue to inspire builders.

Before I can make Michael Lichter's oil lines, I need to mount his oil filter. I used to always run the early-style original canister-type oil filters, instead of the spin-on type. I thought that was hardcore and cool, until the early filter on my 1949 Pan fell off while I was going 85 miles per hour on the interstate last summer. I lunched the engine, and swore off the old filter style. I noticed for years that Indian Larry used the automotive remote-mounted spin-on filters, and decided that if they were good enough for him, they would be good enough for me.

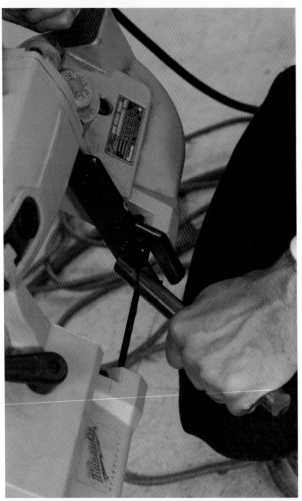

I make the mounts from 1/2-inch-diameter steel round stock. Full of oil, the filter will be pretty heavy, so I need strong mounts for it. Here, I cut the steel stock with my Milwaukee portable band saw.

I TIG weld the oil filter mount to the frame, just behind the transmission. The filter needs to be close to the oil tank and engine so I can make the oil lines as short as possible. Longer lines will result in low oil pressure, which is not good.

Here is a close-up of a finned oil filter mount, with oil line fittings installed.

I make my oil lines from copper tubing used to supply refrigerator icemakers with water. I buy mine at Ace Hardware.

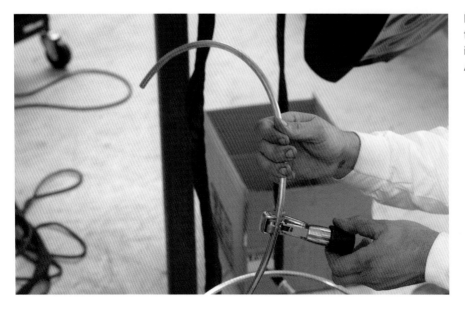

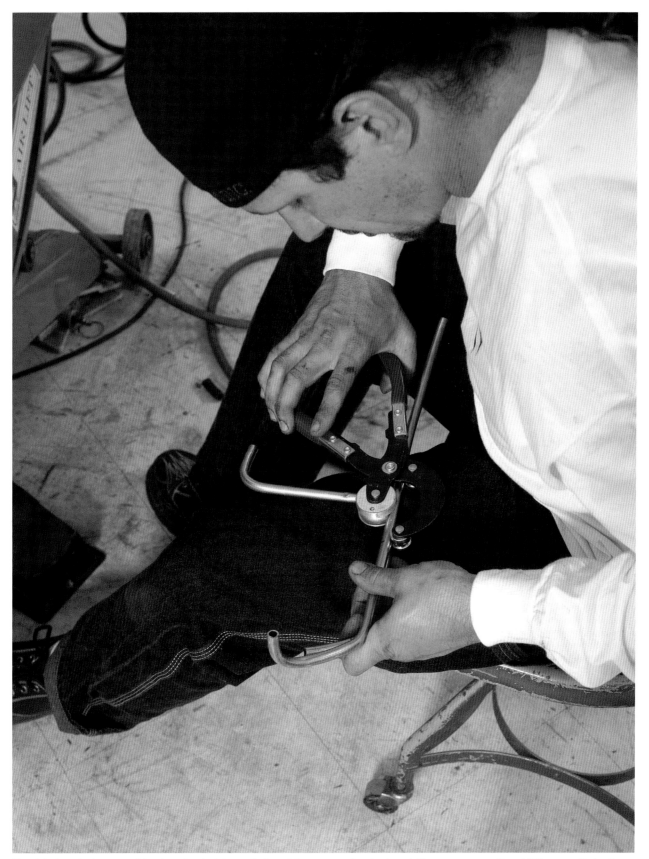

For tight bends I use a tubing bender, but I usually bend the copper line by hand. Some guys use flared fittings on their oil lines, but I prefer to use rubber ends.

This shot shows the oil return-to-tank line installed with rubber ends. Using screw-type flare fittings will inevitably crack the oil lines, due to vibration. The rubber lines absorb the vibrations produced by the big twin engine and make it easy to remove the oil lines for servicing and emergency repairs. This method is also inexpensive, and it has a very race-influenced look.

## Lighting

Shorter rear fenders eventually forced the relocation of the taillight and license tag mount from over the center of the rear wheel to other locations. I have always liked them on the side of the bike. I typically mount mine on the left side near the rear of the frame. I pick a spot that doesn't interfere with the exhaust location or the passenger foot peg location. With a step drill, I bore a 3/4-inch hole in the frame tube to allow the running light and brake light wires to be run through. After miter-cutting a piece of 1-inch frame tubing with a hole saw on my Bridgeport, I place the mitered end over the hole I drilled in the frame and weld the tube in place. I cut the open end of the tube with a cutting wheel, and weld onto it one of the billet steel license tag mounts we make at Choppers, Inc. I pick an arbitrary angle that looks appealing on the bike, and end up with a tag mount that will outlast most everything else on the bike.

Up front, I prefer to run single traditional round headlights. I've never been into rectangular headlights, or headlights shaped like skulls or cat's eyes. Inexpensive headlight shells, like the bullet-shaped version from Paughco, work on any bike. I also use quite a few automobile spot-lamp shells for headlights. Unity is the biggest name I know of, and I have found many different varieties from them with the names of different automotive manufacturers stamped or etched on the top of the shell. They look great, and have plenty of character.

On springers, I always mount the headlight from the spring perch very close to the top springs. I mount the headlight to the bottom fork tree on hydraulic front ends.

My favorite shape is a more expensive billet shell from Arlen Ness. A Ness light looks so incredible between a set of Wide Glide trees at 45 degrees rake. It is a classic look.

Final assembly is critical to the road-worthiness of any custom bike. I always sit down and formulate a plan before beginning work. I like to lay out all my parts, just to make sure I have everything I need and that nothing has been forgotten.

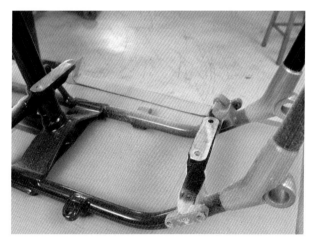

**Above:** Surfaces to be cleaned include the engine mounting pads, transmission mounting pads, foot control mounting points, gas tank mounts, and the like.

**Left:** The first thing I do is remove the paint from any surface that will have a metal-to-metal contact surface.

61

Another important initial step in final assembly is tapping any threaded holes on the bike. Sandblasting, bodywork dust, powdercoating, polishing compound, and chrome plating find their way into threaded holes and can cause seized bolts and disaster.

I like to pull all necessary wires through the frame before installing any of the bike's major components.

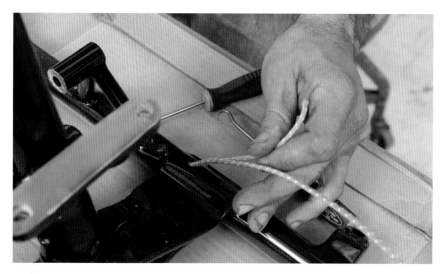

This detail shot shows the taillight and brake light wires coming through the painted frame at the reinforced crossmember.

I install the mechanical drum brake assembly that Joe painted for me. Painting parts like this requires a complete disassembly of the part, then a reassembly prior to installation.

**Next page:** I use high-strength threadlocker to mount everything to the bike. Here, I apply threadlocker to the fender mount.

As always, I'm working from the rear of the bike to the front.

I install the driveline in the order that I lined it up. The transmission goes in and, if my fabrication is well done, the two drive sprockets will line up perfectly.

I install the mechanical rear brake linkage while there are no obstacles in the way—such as an engine, transmission, or primary drive. It is important to make sure these parts work freely and properly at this stage.

It is clear in this photo that Jerry's bobber is progressing nicely. Notice the clean foot control mounts, the wires running through the frame, the suicide clutch cable, and the brake linkage all in place.

I install the chrome-plated oil tank. This is a close fit, so the oil tank needs to go in before the rear wheel.

I also need to install the sissy bar before the rear wheel goes in the bike.

Take a look at Joe Richardson's amazing paint job. I always bring Joe over to look at the bike prior to paint, so he can get a feel for it. Then I give him a general idea of how I want the paint to look. Joe takes over after that and delivers an awesome job every time.

I install the fork neck cups and bearings. I am ready to assemble and install the front fork assembly, then get the bike up on its wheels.

Warlock Willie dropped by to help me install the forks in the frame.

I have to install the handlebars before I install the handmade gas tank I pounded out for Jerry. Jerry's tank hangs forward, way over the handlebars.

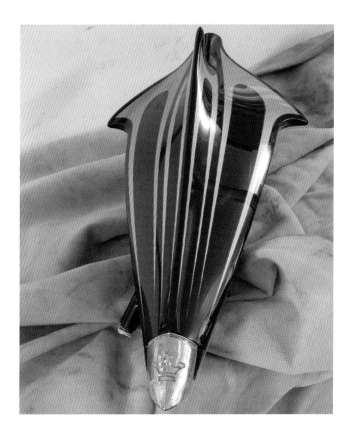

I used part of a taillight from an old Plymouth to finish off the tail of Jerry's tank. I didn't rechrome it because I like the antique look.

I carefully install Jerry's gas tank. Notice how the filler neck and panel below it hang way over the front fork and handlebars.

I decided to run a headlamp and two spots on Jerry's springer. Several bikes were set up this way in the movie *The Wild One*. The headlight is actually an old car spotlamp that my dad bought for $3 at a yard sale. I decided not to rechrome the shell. I had Joe paint and pinstripe the spot shells.

I lace up Jerry's wheels with stainless spokes and set them up in my wheel truing stand.

I center the rims relative to the hub by checking each side of the wheel against the hub's edges with a straight ruler. The wheels will invariably be off-center, so I pull them into the shape using the spokes and some knowledge.

I tighten the spokes methodically, removing the side runout.

For a guy who hates to measure, I sure do enough of it. I use a dial indicator on the edge of the rim to check side runout. I like to get my side runout to within 0.005 inch. That is well within factory specs.

Once I am happy with my side runout, I check the radial runout. This is the hard part of truing spoke wheels, and this is where most people fail. Again, I like my wheels within 0.005-inch radial runout.

When my wheels have been trued, I sign them and date them. When you do good work, you should be proud of it. This is my way of standing behind my quality. The slash marks between the spokes and the numeral "1" are references I use to true the wheel methodically.

I hand mount Jerry's tires the way my dad showed me as a kid. No expensive tire machines for me.

I roll Jerry's front wheel and tire into the stand between the springer rockers to install the axle and spacers. Once I have the wheel in, I can clamp the tire in my lift's cycle vise for stability.

I don't always drink beer on break. Ken and I talk vintage shotguns.

I install the rear wheel to complete the roller.

I check the rear wheel alignment with a vernier caliper.

To complete the rear portion of the driveline, I cut Jerry's chain to length and install it.

With the rear drive chain installed, I am able to lock down Jerry's rear axle and axle adjusting bolts and jam nuts.

I install Jerry's floorboards and kickstand. Everything gets high-strength threadlocker.

I move on to installing the clutch assembly to the transmission's mainshaft. I am progressing forward with the driveline.

It is time for Jerry's Panhead to go into the frame. The engine is the last major component to go in. After this, everything else is just small details.

**Above:** I chose this shot of the rear mechanical brake linkage to illustrate how heavy duty things need to be. Notice the steel mount I welded to the frame behind the brake link. It is from the Builder's Kit, and securely mounts the transmission to the frame on the left side. Since I am running no primary backing plate on this bike, these mounts will provide extra reinforcement for the five-speed.

**Left:** I tighten down the engine mount bolts. These things need to be tight. As an old graybeard biker told me a long time ago when I was still wet behind the ears, "Tighten them down until they squeak—then give them another quarter turn."

Installing the primary belt drive.

Even though I've probably checked it 10 times, I still make another primary driveline check with a straight ruler. I always want to know that my fab work has been done right.

I need to install the generator to finish up the electric wiring. The last things to do are to install the oil lines and throttle cable, add the fluids, and fire her up.

## Wheels and Tires

There are so many variations of wheels and tires that there should be a book dedicated to just that. I personally think that custom billet wheels have gotten out of control. An inordinate number of manufacturers are building wheels that are surprisingly similar in style. When it comes to billet wheels, I have always stuck with simple cuts like Extreme Machine's Blade or Performance-Machine's Villain designs. Tom Langton made a cool set of "Dice-N-Trucker Girl" wheels for me out of billet aluminum that we designed together. Only one set exists, on the Biker Build-Off bike that I built to ride with Indian Larry during the summer of 2003, but I figured there would be a thousand copycat sets on the street within months. That never happened, much to my amazement.

Billet wheel styles will come and go, but we will always find choppers and bobbers rolling on spokes. I got

my start in the spoke wheel business over 10 years ago, and have a loyalty to them. It is very salty near the ocean in Florida where we live. Because of that, I like my wheels two ways: powder-coated hubs and rims with stainless spokes, or polished stainless rims and hubs with stainless spokes. Landmark and Buchanan make the best stainless spokes—they don't experience thread gall when I try to true the wheel.

If I do happen to use chrome wheels and hubs, I take them to Space Coast Plating, near my shop in Melbourne. The quality work they do to my metal lasts long after the pain from the cost of plating already-plated wheels fades away. Besides, the downtime and labor of having to remove the wheels and tires from the bike, relacing and retruing, balancing, and putting it back on the road, is the worst fate imaginable.

# CHAPTER FIVE
## SHEET METAL

## Gas Tanks

One of the first things I look for in a bike are cool, classic lines. Whether it is a chopper or a bobber, poor lines are a total deal breaker. And nothing has the ability to disrupt the lines of a bike like a poorly shaped or misplaced gas tank. I have been told that I create notoriously wild and unique gas tanks, so I pour all of my pride into every one.

The foundation for a great gas tank is the tunnel. The tunnel is the U-shaped section that drapes over the backbone of the frame the way a towel rests over a rack. To me, it is important to keep the tunnel fairly close to the frame's backbone. I usually bend a piece of flat 16-gauge steel over a piece of pipe to create my tunnels. If my frame has a 1 1/2-inch-diameter backbone, I shove a piece of 1 3/4-inch-diameter frame tubing into a pipe vise and bend the sheet over that.

Once the tunnel is formed, it is time to locate and install the tank mounts. I build small tanks, typically between 2- and 3-gallon capacity. Because of their small capacity, I am able to get away with a very simple mounting system. I drill into the frame's backbone and weld in three counterbored and drilled mounts from a Choppers, Inc. Builder's Kit. It is generally best to place two of the mounts toward the front of the frame, and the third near the rear of the backbone, since custom chopper gas tanks usually hold most of their fuel in their forward area. I install bolts in the three mounts, and screw a threaded bung from the Builder's Kit onto each one.

Next, I put a dab of grease on each bung. This is the method I use to transfer the location of each mount on the frame onto the tunnel. By carefully placing the tunnel over

I begin work on the gas tank by forming the tunnel and the floor. Prior to doing this, I need to measure the frame's backbone to see how long I can make the tank.

I lay the tunnel and floor out on sheet metal with a Sharpie. The two solid lines I scribed are where the bends of the tunnel will be. The dotted line denotes the centerline of the tunnel. It is only for reference. Here the sheet metal is placed in the bending brake, ready for bending.

the mounts, the grease adheres to the under surface of the tunnel. I remove the tunnel, turn it so that its undersurface is facing up, and drill holes for the bungs at each grease mark. Once the holes are correctly drilled, I place the tunnel back over the frame and align the holes in the tunnel with the three bungs. Prior to welding, it is important to clean away the grease, as it will grossly contaminate the weld. Once the bungs are welded to the tunnel, the tunnel is firmly in place over the frame. The last thing to do is to plug the top of each bung with a short button-head bolt. I weld around the perimeter of the head of the bolt, forming a seal with the bung. I have forgotten to do this in the past, creating the need to completely open up a virtually finished gas tank that would have leaked profusely.

Depending on whether the tank will hang down below the frame's backbone, or sit above it Frisco style, there may be steps that need to be taken with the tunnel prior to welding in the mounts. If going with the Frisco Style, I bend the tunnel up 90 degrees on each side, creating the bottom panel or floor of the gas tank. This is how I generally make my tanks, with a flat bottom and Frisco Style mounting.

Two huge considerations with gas tanks are capacity and interference. I always try to make my tanks as long as possible in order to increase fuel capacity. This tends to lead to interference with the handlebars, which often influence the shapes and designs of my tanks. My method of creating tanks is to go in with a general idea of the lines I want and where I want my concave and convex spaces to be. However, I don't restrict myself by being too picky. If I start working a shape, and it digresses from my original plan, I usually go where the metal takes me. Sometimes it takes me to a better place, and sometimes I have to manipulate it through force.

It would require too much space to fully explore the metal forming techniques needed to build a nice gas tank, and there are several good books already on the shelves that do just that. I usually cut the panels and preform them over my knee or a piece of pipe to achieve the general shape I am looking for. If my shape requires compound curves, I create them with metal-forming hammers and a leather bag filled with lead shot. When I need very tight curves, I prefer to use my pneumatic planishing hammer. I roll the lumps out of the metal with the English wheel.

I bend both sides of the tunnel in the bending brake, one side at a time.

I've built some extreme shapes without ever utilizing the English wheel, and I've built some tanks with up to 19 panels where every inch of the tank has been hammered and rolled. Often, I'll begin to bend my tank panels and tack them in place. I use the heat from the tack welds to work the metal into shapes I'd never be able to pull at room temperature. Some people tack weld an entire tank together first, then go back and do the final stitching. I like to tack some, then stitch specific areas to build some rigidity from which to work.

It is difficult to teach style, but many of my tanks have a few unique features that set them apart from the pack. These days, everyone is trying to hide everything on their bikes. I say if something is ugly, hide it. But if it is beautiful, show it off. Or if something is ugly, make it beautiful. I look at a gas cap the way old car makers looked at radiator caps. They were the centerpiece of the vehicle. On many of my bikes, I've used antique radiator caps for gas caps. Sometimes, I build the gas tank around the gas cap. I let the gas cap dictate to me what the rest of the tank will look like. Instead of just placing the cap horizontally in the middle of the tank, I will cock it to one side, or rake it forward at an angle. Other times, I weld a piece of frame tubing to the tank to create a filler neck, almost looking like a military jet's in-flight refueling nozzle. Several times I have placed the gas tank on the frame, right up against the top of the forks. When I turned the handlebars, they hit the tank. So I made cut-out reliefs in the tank to accommodate the bars. I love that look.

Most of my tanks are pretty narrow toward the rear. There isn't a whole lot of space inside between the walls of the tank and the tunnel. And the rear of the tank is where the petcock needs to go. I usually make a petcock fitting out of a piece of frame tubing that I weld to the rear of the tank on the left side. This method virtually eliminates the ability to use the reserve valve on the petcock, so be prepared to push your bike from time to time.

The tunnel looks like a long channel, but it is actually inverted.

Ken and I laugh about something that probably has nothing to do with the gas tank I need to make. However, the tunnel is in position the way it will actually sit on the frame.

To bend the tunnel, we place the sheet metal channel over a piece of steel pipe exactly as it was positioned in the last photo.

With the tunnel and floor panel bent, I drill holes for the gas tank mounts in the tunnel with a step drill.

The gas tank mounts are from the Choppers, Inc. Builder's Kit. I TIG weld them in, and plug the top of them with Allen bolts. I TIG weld the Allen bolt plugs to the mounts to ensure a good seal.

Now that I have the tunnel and floor in place on the bike, I lay out a general plan for the shape of the bike onto the floor with a Sharpie.

**Above:** I remove the panel I don't want using my band saw. I only remove one side at first, just to be sure I'm happy with the shape I have chosen.

**Left:** I clamp the floor to my welding table to ensure that it stays flat as I weld to it.

**Below:** I made templates for the two side panels and cut them out on the band saw. I bend them over my knee to achieve the desired curvature and shape. I make both of these panels simultaneously for easy duplication.

It will take a little bit of tweaking to get my side panel to match the contour of the floor panel, so I bend it to fit. Once I know it fits correctly, I trim the other side of the gas tank floor and tweak the other side panel to match.

I begin attaching the side panels to the floor by tack welding a few choice spots around the tank.

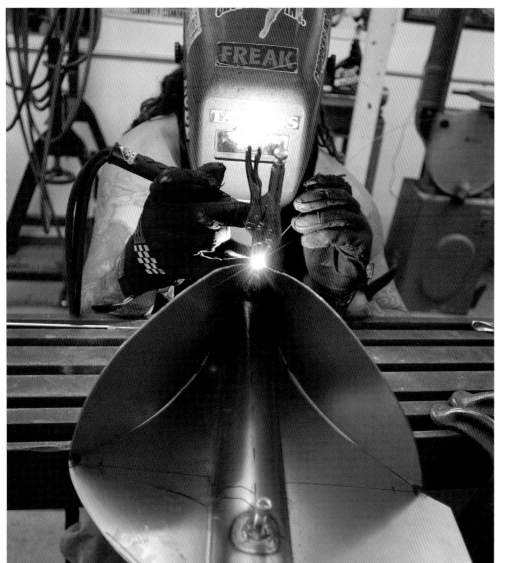

Here is a shot looking in from the front of the tank. The gaps on either side of the tank between the floor and the side panels were caused by the heat of my tack welds. I'll have to tap the sides in with a mallet to close those gaps prior to welding.

Once I get the sides to fit the floor the way I want them to, I tack along the bottom joint. This seam is the most critical one to weld. It takes the greatest abuse, due to the weight of the fuel it will hold.

Usually, several times during fabrication, I like to mount the tank on the bike. Having the uncompleted tank on the bike allows me to note my progress and pick the direction I want to go with the shape. It is also much easier to grind my welded seams down with the tank bolted down.

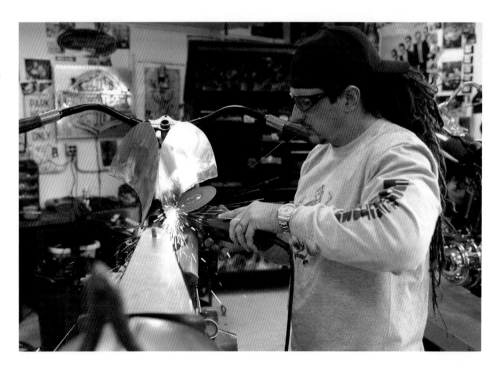

I make another paper template to fit the front quarters of the gas tank. The templates get me very close to where I need to be in fit and shape, but they are not exact.

**Above:** It usually takes me several attempts and test fittings to bend the panels over my leg and get a good fit on the panels.

**Left:** I bend the front quarter panels over my leg to roughly shape them.

When the panel is bent to what I think will make a close fit, I tack weld it on. Note the relief for the gas tank tunnel on the quarter panel. I tack first at the furthest point from the tunnel, and work toward it. I use the heat introduced to the sheet metal to manipulate the panel and work it into shape.

This is a great shot of me performing a tack weld while pulling the panel into shape with my left hand. As I pull on the panel, I feel a springy resistance. As soon as the welding heat travels through the metal to my hand, I can feel that resistance release itself.

Metal stretches from bending and heat. Now my quarter panel overlaps the centerline of the gas tank, so I lay my paper template over the panel and mark where the centerline should be. I trim the template, flip it over, and transfer the shape to create the quarter panel for the other side.

After I weld on the second quarter panel, there is a little bit of trimming to do with a cutting wheel.

I finish weld the other quarter panel to the side panel and floor to give the tank some structure and rigidity.

Now that I have the general shape of the gas tank laid out, I finish grind all of my welds and move on to the real details of the tank.

*Bobzilla's* gas cap is going to be a 1923 Plymouth radiator cap. I want to run the cap with a hard forward rake, because I think it gives the bike an aggressive attitude.

The Plymouth radiator cap has a bayonet-type locking mechanism to keep it attached, so I cut a bayonet-type receptacle from an old gas tank from my junk pile and weld it to a piece of exhaust pipe.

The exhaust pipe will serve as my filler neck.

The filler neck is too long, so I cut it with a fiber cutting disc.

I set the filler neck on top of the tank and mark the spot with a Sharpie where I want it to penetrate the tank.

**Above:** I make one last check before welding the filler neck in—placement is critical. It needs to be at the highest point of the tank to deliver maximum fuel capacity, and it has to look good.

**Left:** I cut the hole for the filler neck with a pneumatic reciprocating saw from the mark I made.

**Below:** As I TIG weld the filler neck into the top of the tank, the aggressive stance of the Plymouth cap becomes apparent against the angles of the handlebars. It's gonna look good.

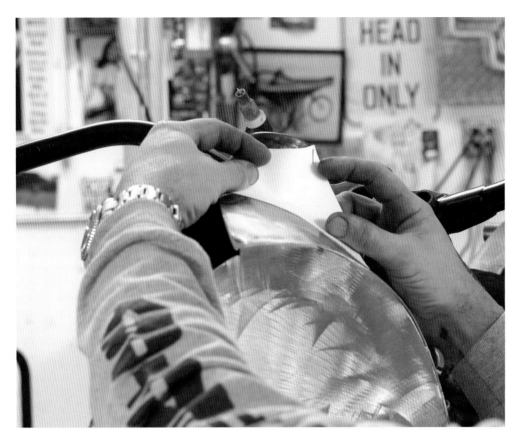

Though it's tricky, I make a couple of paper templates for the small steel panels that will hide the ugly filler neck I made.

A view of the small filler panel tack welded to the filler neck. The panel is so small that I don't even try to prebend it. I just tack weld it to the tank, and use the heat from the welds to manipulate it.

This shot clearly shows how I tack and bend the steel panel into shape.

With Vise Grips, I clamp the panel to the other side and visually check for alignment and symmetry. It won't ever be perfect, but that's fine with me.

Here is a nice shot of me welding the small panels in place. What's nice about it is that it shows the difference between the completed right side and the unfinished left. The change in shape and positioning of those panels is dramatic before and after my welding and hammering operation. I think the symmetry of that tank against the handlebars is remarkable.

With the tank off the bike, I finish tapping the small panels into position and weld them down for good.

I grind my welds away as I go. It makes it much easier to finish the tank off if I grind as I go. The tank has really taken shape with the addition of the filler neck and panels.

I have decided to create some negative space in the area behind the filler neck by adding four small panels. This is the template for two of them.

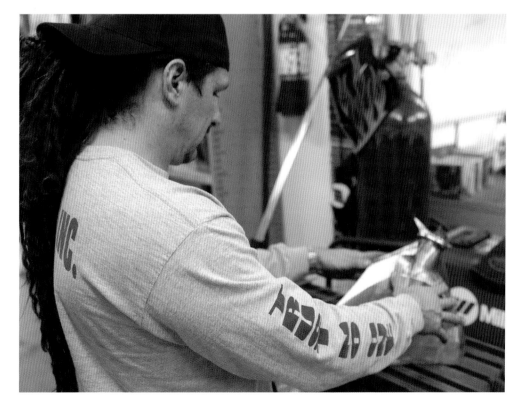

The third panel is pretty complex. It will be a negative recess that opens outward, much as the pages of this book do near the binding.

The close-up shot of the paper template for the recessed panel shows one of the two matching small filler panels welded in place.

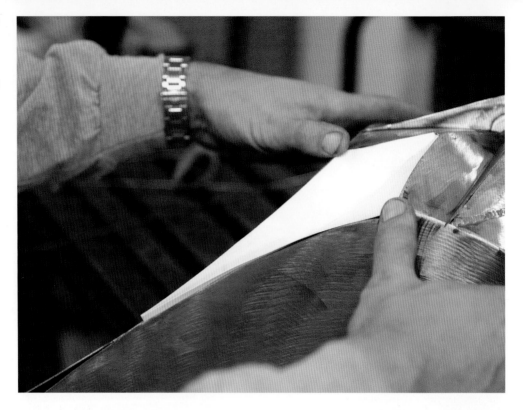

I cut the blank for the recessed panel on the band saw. The black line down the middle is where I will bend the panel.

I bend the blank for the recessed panel in my bending brake.

The bent recessed panel starts out looking like this.

I gently bend out the sides of the recessed panel to fit the opening in the tank.

I hold the panel down in the tank with the end of my sheetmetal hammer and begin to tack weld it into position.

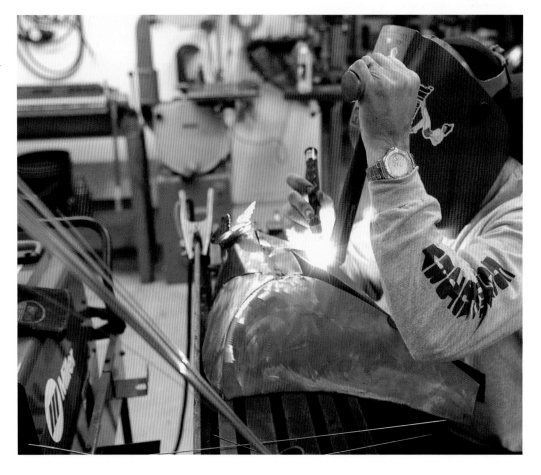

Notice how well the panel fits on the right side. Once again, I used the heat from the tack welds and a metal mallet to force the panel into its final shape.

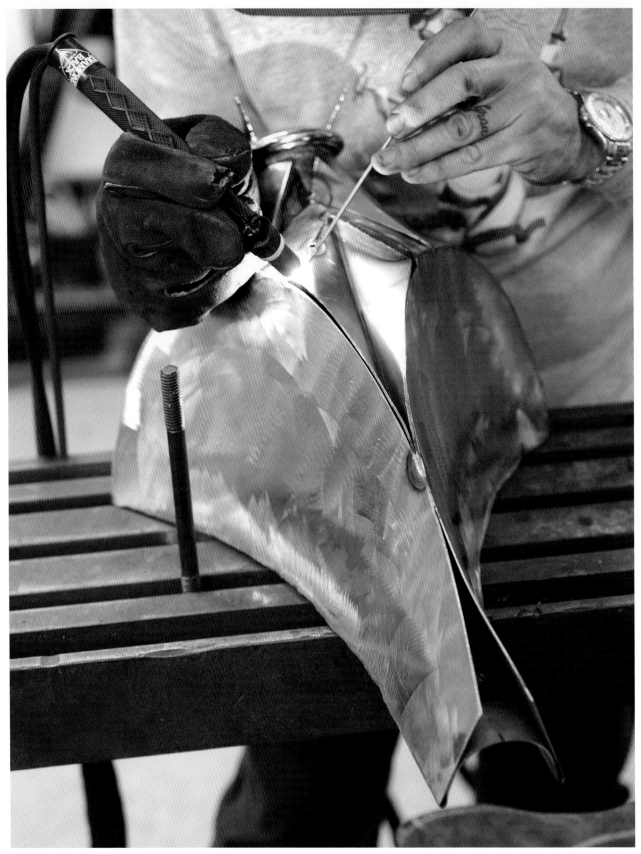

Note the difference in fitment of the recessed panel between this photo and the previous one. As soon as I finish this tack weld, I will pound the panel's edge down with my mallet and the seam will be tight enough to finish weld.

To fill the gap in the rear of the tank, I make a panel much like the one I just finished.

## Fenders

Before I build a gas tank that will give a bike hot looks, I have to know what the rear fender looks like. As I mentioned with driveline setup, I always work from the rear of the bike toward the front. Same goes for the aesthetics of the sheet metal. I need to know, before I start with the fender, where the rear wheel will sit in the frame when the rear chain or belt is tight, because I cut the fenders extremely close to the tire. A small slip-up here can cost me hours of trouble later.

I typically use Jesse James' fenders, or those spun by my friend A. J. at Lucky's Choppers in Washington State. I buy A. J.'s fenders as complete donuts, which allows me lots of freedom in cutting and shaping the finished product. The key is to select a fender with a width 1 inch wider than the tire (when mounted on the rim). This selection, minus the thickness of the fender, provides roughly 3/8 inch on either side of the tire. I run my rear fenders very short. Don't believe the hype—chopper fenders don't exist to keep road dirt and rain off the rider. They exist so the honeys have a place to sit. That is why I never run front fenders on my chops and bobbers. Front fenders are just more shit to be painted and scratched. Save the fender money and spend it on a good custom seat.

From the center of the rear axle to the edge of the tire, I pick a radius where I'd like to see the fender ride. Generally, I choose the point where the sidewall and the tread surface meet. I transfer this radius to both sides of the fender blank using an adjustable square and a Sharpie pen. Some guys

Lucky's fender blank has too much side material for my taste. I use a compound square and a Sharpie to mark my desired radius. I place the edge of the square on the existing radius, and adjust the scale so that the end of it is at the radius I wish to cut. There is a provision at the end of the scale that gives the point of my Sharpie a place to rest. By placing the Sharpie here and sliding the edge of the square along the fender's inner radius, I am able to scribe a mark denoting the new radius.

Lucky's fender blank has too much side material for my taste. I use a compound square and a Sharpie to mark my desired radius. I place the edge of the square on the existing radius, and adjust the scale so that the end of it is at the radius I wish to cut. There is a provision at the end of the scale that gives the point of my Sharpie a place to rest. By placing the Sharpie here and sliding the edge of the square along the fender's inner radius, I am able to scribe a mark denoting the new radius.

like the look of a fender that runs all the way down toward the ground in front of the tire. I don't. This can cause huge chain and belt adjustment problems down the road, and problems mean less fun. I tend to cut my fenders short just beyond where the top rear frame legs cross the tire in the front. If we call the very top point of the rear tire 12 o'clock, I cut my fenders off at 1 o'clock at the rear, and around 10 o'clock toward the front.

The total length of the fender I choose is called, in geometry, an arc length. Whatever arc length I choose, I mark the fender at the spot I'd like it to begin and end. I lay the fender flat on the ground on its side. Then, using a length of TIG welding rod, I form the rod into an L-shape. What I have is a crude plumb-bob. By cutting the TIG rod at the appropriate length, I am able to hang it from the upper side of the fender and locate the exact beginning point and ending point on the other side of the fender. Gravity can be your best friend or your worst enemy—and it is a very unforgiving enemy. The key is to find a balance between the two. Mark the other side of the fender with the Sharpie, and it is time to cut both the radius and the entire arc length away from the donut.

I use a reciprocating saw, or sometimes a plasma cutter, to create the radius. I always use a 7-inch cutting wheel to cut across the fender. I penetrate the disc into the fender to its core. This deep penetration provides me with a virtual straightedge, insuring a square cut laterally across the fender. I always wear heavy leather gloves when cutting and handling a raw rear fender. The cutting disc leaves a gnarly edge, and I have more scars on my palms from being a gloveless jackass than from anything else. It is important to de-burr all of the edges of the fender with an abrasive disc or file prior to proceeding.

Positioning and mounting the fender is a tough job, but I use a pretty crude method to get it done. Using a towel placed between the tire and fender, doubled or tripled over, I find a thickness that gives me a very snug fender fit over the tire. It is important, at this point, to realize that the fender will flex quite a bit under normal riding. If your honey on the back has had a couple of tequila shots, it's going to flex even more. There has to be ample space between the tire and fender at their closest distance, or you'll be buying another paint job and listening to her whine about her blistered ass. I've been there.

The Sharpie rests nicely in the end of the square's scale. I scribe the new radius on both sides of the fender.

Taking the gamble that I have the fender placed well above the tire, I line it up with the bike by eye. Either you have it or you don't. If you don't, make friends with someone who has that kind of eye. It used to be that I'd mount my fenders to the frame's seat cross bar in front of the rear tire, but I have changed my ways. For a while now, I have been mounting the front of the fender just beneath the frames upper legs. I weld two of the 5/16-inch threaded bungs from a Choppers, Inc. Builder's Kit to the fender at each of the front corners. Using two of the counterbored slugs from the Builder's Kit, I thread bolts into the bungs on the fender. The best way I have found to affix the slugs to the frame for welding is using clamps and V-blocks from my machine shop. However, I've done it using Vise-Grips before, and I've even used bungee cords. Welding heat has a brutal effect on bungee cords, though. And they smell when they burn.

A large Vernier caliper works great to align the fender mounts on each side of the frame, but not everyone has one lying around. Before I bought mine, I used a piece of TIG rod. Using the center of the rear axle as a reference, I cut a length of TIG rod 2 inches longer than I need. Making a mark 1 inch from each end, I bend it 90 degrees at each

mark. This simple piece of steel rod is the gauge that I use to ensure my mounts line up.

The final step in mounting a rear fender is to build the sissy bar. Sissybars kind of went out of style in the mid-1990s when Jesse James smacked the world up with his revolutionary tire-hugging fender shapes. Jesse's fender shapes mimicked the tire contour so well that I can't say I blame him for not wanting to interrupt that relationship by including a sissy bar. Everyone followed suit, or so it seemed.

I had always considered a sissy bar a virtual necessity on a bike. Though I've done a few bikes without them, I prefer to make a statement with mine. Besides looking cool, they are great to tie things to, and keep the ladies on board when the clutch goes out fast. I used to make simple, triangular sissybars out of straight steel bar stock. If a bike had 45 degrees of rake, I would mount the sissy bar at 45 degrees of rake. It is a good look, but difficult to pull off with a short rear fender. I started heating and bending the bar stock, creating curved sissybars that provided the illusion of intense rake without having to lay the bar back so much. My shapes have become more intricate in the last couple of years. I have started to shape the sissy bar so that, when viewed from behind, the lines of the bar seem to flow into the lines of the tank.

I have to cut the fender to the proper length from the blank. Once I have determined that length, I need to mark it on one side and transfer it to the other. It is pretty difficult to transfer the mark from one side to the other, across the big radius in the fender. I have devised a simple method. I bend a piece of TIG welding filler rod 90 degrees to form a type of plum bob. When I lay the plum bob at the mark on one side of the fender, it indicates the spot on the opposite side of the fender where I need to make my cut.

I mark the spot at the end of my plum bob with a Sharpie.

I will cut the fender with my Miller plasma cutter. To make a smooth, radiused cut, I lightly clamp a set of Vise-Grips to the handle of the plasma torch. The vise grips will serve as a guide as they follow the inner radius of the fender blank.

I make a couple of trial passes with the plasma torch before I pull the trigger, just to get used to the feeling of the Vise-Grip guide against the fender.

Once I feel comfortable, I pull the trigger and let the plasma cut, as I follow the inside radius of the fender with the Vise-grips. Note the clean cut the Miller makes as I go.

Following the marks I made on the fender with the Sharpie, Eric removes the unwanted side material with the plasma.

With both side sections removed, Eric runs a piece of masking tape across the radius of the fender. The masking tape is a visual guide for Eric as he cuts with a fiber cutting disc on the 7-inch angle grinder. Note the huge reduction in side coverage due to our plasma cutting.

Eric removes our fender from the remainder of the blank.

**Left:** Eric removes the slag produced from the plasma cut with a grinding disc.

**Below:** Eric takes the roughly finished fender we have cut and checks it over the rear tire for fitment. The tighter that fender fits the tire, the better *Bobzilla* will look.

To place the fender as close as possible to the tire without the risk of contact between the two, I double over an old T-shirt and lay it between the fender and tire. I measure from the rear of the frame to the front of the fender to determine placement of my fender mounts.

The fender mounts have to be extremely strong, because I plan to haul young women around on the back of my bikes. I use billet steel parts from a Choppers, Inc. Builder's Kit to secure the fender to the frame. I like the mounts to align with the frame, so I use a couple of V-blocks from my machine shop and a C-clamp to hold them in place while I weld.

I TIG weld the front fender mounts on both sides of the bike. The rear of the fender will be supported by one of my custom sissy bars.

With the fender secured to the bike, Eric ensures that the rear lip of the fender is evenly cut. He makes minor adjustments with a sanding disc.

It is time to make the sissy bar, an important visual part of any chopper. I use 5/8-inch diameter cold-rolled steel bar stock, which is extremely difficult to bend. In order to make the bends I want, I use the heat from my oxygen-acetylene torches.

The goal with the torches is to cause the section of the steel stock I want to bend to become red hot. This takes a few minutes.

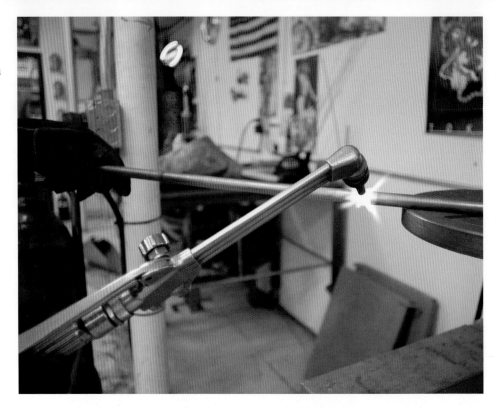

The table of my drill press just happens to be the exact radius I need for my sissy bar to mimic the radius of the Lucky's fender correctly. The heated metal bends rather easily.

I need to include a dogleg on the primary side of the bike to clear the chain. I do this by putting the sissy bar in a vise, heating with the acetylene torch, then bending the bar until it forms the correct angles.

Eric holds the sissy bar in place while I clamp the mounts from the Builder's Kit to the bar. Once everything is in place, I'll TIG weld the mounts to the bar and to the frame.

I TIG weld a set of mounts from the Builder's Kit to the sissy bar and to the fender.

With the rear mounts firmly welded to the fender and sissy bar, the fender is securely fastened to the bike. This is the function part. I can move on to the form part of the sissy bar now.

I weld a short piece of steel stock to each side of the sissy bar. The steel is still hot from the welding, so a quick shot from the acetylene torch makes them easy to bend. I use a box-end wrench to provide leverage for bending. Take care to make sure the final position matches from side to side or your sissy bar will look unbalanced.

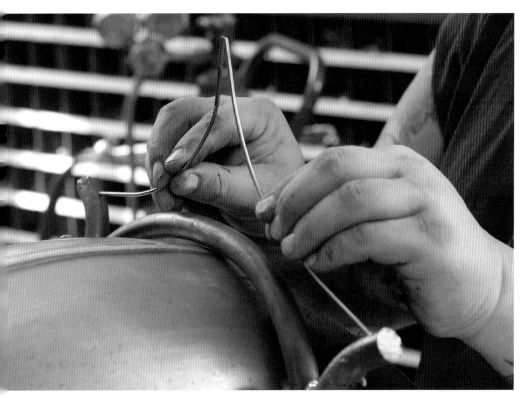

Using TIG filler rod, we make a wire template to which we will bend the final two pieces of the sissy bar. The wire template basically serves as a guide, so we know if our bends are too tight or too loose.

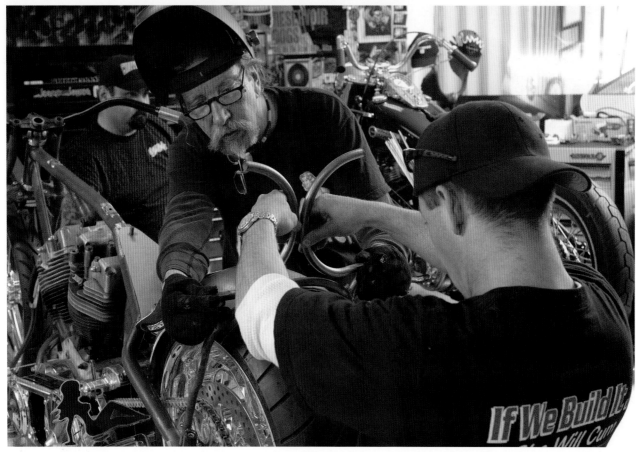

Ken and Eric bend the last two pieces of the sissy bar according to the wire templates. I wanted the bends as tight and smooth as possible.

When the bends were right, Ken TIG welded everything together.

Eric removes excess material from the bar stock with a cutting disc. This paves the way for him to finish the shape of the sissy bar with a sanding disc.

Here is a detail shot of the unfinished sissy bar. Note that the right side has been filled and finished to shape. The left side still needs to be filled. The center section has yet to be trimmed, filled, or finished.

This is what the finished sissy bar looks like.

Another view of the completed sissy bar.

Eric sanding and shaping the aluminum piece that will become one of my rear axle covers.

Here I hold up an unfinished aluminum wing and mark the axle cover for positioning.

A marked axle cover showing where I'm going to weld the wing in place.

Lining up both axle covers to make sure my marks are symetric.

I clamp the wing and the axle cover together on the welding table so I can tack weld them together.

**Below:** Here I TIG weld the two aluminum pieces together on the welding table.

Here I visually check the symetry of the two axle covers after welding.

The axle cover mounted on *Bobzilla*. Note that the wings don't need to be contoured—they're still unfinished.

Ken marks where he plans to grind a set of steel wings that will be mounted on *Bobzilla's* fork neck gussets.

With an angle grinder Ken begins to shape the wings.

Ken finishes contouring the steel wings with an angle grinder and sanding disc. Once the wings are fully stripped they'll be chrome plated and welded to the steering neck prior to painting the frame.

I decided to make dual pipes for Michael Lichter's bobber. Duals, by my definition, are a set of pipes with one exiting each side of the bike, versus the conventional way Harley-Davidson makes them: exiting on the right side of the bike. I always start with the rear exhaust pipe, since the pipe exits the head in such close proximity to the frame's seat post and oil tank. The greatest risk for interference is at the rear exhaust port, and I always like to do the hardest work first.

## Exhaust

If you are a horsepower freak, skip over the following. It will upset you. I make custom exhaust systems to make my bikes look good. I rarely consider performance at all. V-twin engines are so inefficient that we have gone nuts building them bigger and bigger. Increasing displacement really is the only way to produce any real horsepower with street tunability. I build them to look good, and I'm willing to sacrifice a few horses for style's sake.

It is easiest to begin with spigots from a used set of exhausts. I always start by fastening the 1 3/4-inch spigots to the heads. Often, I have to come right off the head with a tight bend to make the curves I need. I usually run about 8 to 10 inches of 1 3/4-inch-diameter pipe, then step up to 2-inch-diameter all the way back to the tips.

Many builders and manufacturers are now using and making exhaust pipes with smooth radiused curves, like Jesse's HellBent pipes. Arlen Ness did this years ago on one of his streamliner bikes. I've stayed away from that style of pipes for a few reasons, the main one being that everyone jumped on board. Those pipes look good on swoopy-shaped bikes, but I like linear shapes in my bikes. Instead of long, smooth curves, I prefer a combination of varying tight bends and long, straight sections. My style is derived from drag car headers, which bend and change direction to maintain equal pipe length and clear obstacles.

Mounting pipes is an important consideration not to be overlooked. I mount mine in at least three places on each pipe, usually to the frame. Using bungs and counter-bored slugs from the builder's kit, I weld the mounts to points on the frame and pipes that will allow for easy installation and removal. This can be tricky, but the key is to make the pipes strong enough to lift the bike off the ground with.

I chose a random bending mistake from my box of exhaust pipes. The rear pipe will run between the rear head and the seat post, and I have found a section of bent pipe that will work nicely. This is the view from the right side. I am going to have to cut the visible piece off and replace it, since it doesn't line up with the exhaust port.

I will mount the pipe to the frame with a steel slug from the Builder's Kit. Here I hold it in place where I think it should be welded to the frame and pipe.

I weld the threaded slug to the frame's reinforcing plate.

**Left:** I've found another section with a slight bend in it that will work well for the tail end of the rear pipe. The bend in it shoots the pipe outward past the shock absorber of Michael's swing-arm four-speed frame.

With the pipe in position, I weld the tailpipe to the mount on the frame.

This shot illustrates what the rear pipe will roughly look like when finished.

I insert a short, tightly radiused bend into the exhaust port. Note the rear tailpipe section coming across the bike from the other side between the seat post and the rear cylinder head. The trick is to connect these two pieces smoothly.

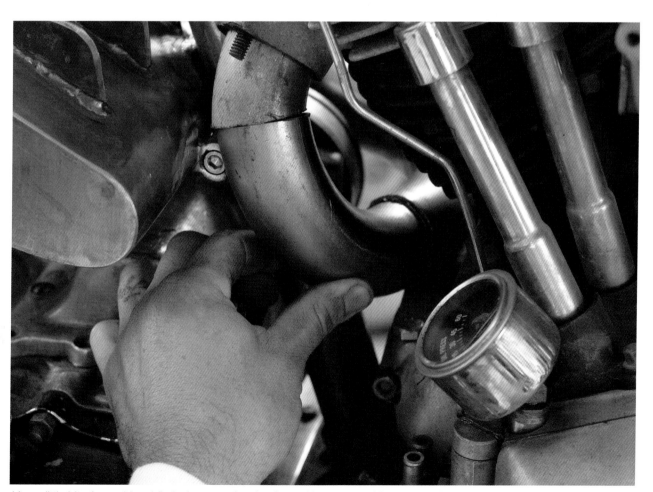

After a little bit of searching, I find a bent section that I am able to cut and fit between the head pipe and tailpipe I have created.

I always consider other options before finalizing a set of pipes. A tricky pipe like this one may be difficult to install and remove from the bike. Here I try another bend right off the head. It doesn't fit right, so I go back to Plan A.

With my Plan A pipe solidly welded together, I rethink the way it is mounted, how the front pipe will match the rear pipe from the other side of the bike, whether the oil tank will clear the rear header pipe, and whether I will be able to route the oil lines in an aesthetically pleasing manner. Note the threaded slug from the Builder's Kit welded to the seat post visible just behind the curve in the header pipe. I weld a mount to the pipe that threads into the slug. This mount, the rear mount, and the exhaust port flange will provide the three mounting points necessary to ensure these pipes will never come loose under any circumstances.

In order to make the front pipe line up with the rear pipe, I measure the height of the rear mount with a square.

I move the square to the opposite side of the bike and position the rear mount for the front pipe into place.

For the time being, I weld the mount to the frame. This will provide me with a reference point from which to work. The pipes will angle upward from the front of the bike to the rear, and getting both pipes to line up is on the tricky side.

Things work against me sometimes. It was going to be impossible to make both pipes line up properly, so I cut the rear pipe and rewelded a section of it. Sometimes I have to work back and forth and from side to side to achieve success.

I try to mentally connect the pipe I have inserted in the front exhaust port with the section I plan to use for the tailpipe. I need to keep in mind that the pipes on both sides of the bike need to line up with each other. The engine provides an obstacle on the right side of the bike that I am going to have to work around.

I cut the rear section and weld it to the rear mount. I'll work from here forward, since the two rear pipes will be the most visible parts of the exhaust.

The cam cover and gear chest of the Shovelhead engine are right in the path of my exhaust pipe. I need to build in a dog leg to clear this part of the engine. I'll make it from two slightly bent short sections of pipe. This means more welding than I anticipated.

I hold the two short bent sections of pipe in place prior to welding. This zigzag in the pipe will actually break up what would have been an extraordinarily long, straight front exhaust pipe. A pipe that long and that straight would kill the lines of Michael's bobber, so the obstacle I encountered has become a welcome surprise.

I TIG weld all of the joints on the front pipe, bouncing around from joint to joint. The alternate welding keeps the pipe from pulling itself out of shape.

I'm not so sure I'm happy with Michael's pipes yet, so I check them out from all angles. They look good, and they are different. But I have to take into consideration the overall bike when finished. I have to ask myself if I can make a gas tank and sissy bar that will look good with these pipes.

At this point I have decided that I am happy with the pipes, and that they will work with my vision of the completed bike. I double check to be sure that they will be functional. They clear the shocks and the oil tank, and they are symmetric to the centerline of the bike.

I make the final welds on the pipes for Michael's bike.

I check and finish all of the welds and mounts. The pipes will experience quite a bit of heat and vibration, and a weak weld will end up cracking under the pressure.

## Foot Controls

Choice and placement of foot controls are important for several reasons. Foot control placement affects the rider's posture, which, as I mentioned when discussing seats, is critical to comfort. Another thing to think about is foot peg height. Pegs that are too low may drag through turns, or cause the heel of the boot to catch the ground.

I prefer forward controls with pegs that are high and a little wider than usual. On long trips, wider pegs allow me to move my legs around a little to keep comfortable. The Choppers, Inc. foot controls I use on my customs are higher than most controls and use wide pegs. Indian Larry liked his forward controls high and narrow for splitting lanes in the city. I'm a big lane splitter also, but I need wide pegs.

The axis that the levers pivot from are the centers of the footpegs. I think this is the most ergonomically correct configuration. It especially helps when riding a bike equipped with a suicide clutch. The natural position of the heel on the peg makes it almost necessary to pivot the levers from this axis. I never understood why some manufacturers would make foot controls that pivot from elsewhere.

In my opinion, true bobbers should have floorboards. Nothing feels better than riding a bobber with a frame-mounted seat and factory floorboards. It feels like I am sitting down in the bike versus sitting up on top of it. The placement of the boards kicks my knees up above my hips, so they're almost touching my elbows. It feels good, because it is good. The boards on my *Hell's Bells* are razor sharp on the edges from years of hard cornering.

This steel pivot from the foot controls has a self-lubricating bronze bushing. The bushing is honed out with a berry-hone so that it pivots freely on its axle.

I am using old connecting rods from a small-block Chevy engine as my foot pedals. The connecting rod is welded to the steel pivot from the previous photo. I've never seen this done before, and I think it will look great.

This shot shows the left side foot control bolted to the frame, with an Arlen Ness kickstand. This side will hold the suicide shift clutch pedal.

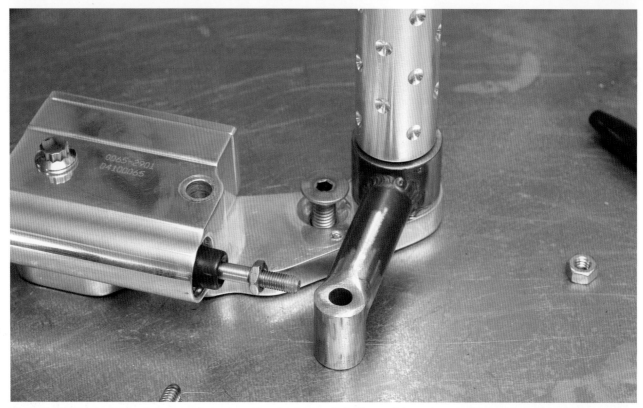

This detail of the brake control shows how strong I make things. *Bobzilla* won't have front brakes, so I need to make sure the rear brakes are dependable. The welds need to be strong, and the steel stock has to be able to handle heavy pedal pressure without bending.

This shot shows the left side foot control bolted to the frame, with an Arlen Ness kickstand. This side will hold the suicide shift clutch pedal.

Every now and then, I take a break.

I build up the welds and ensure that I penetrate deeply beneath the metal's surface. I can't stress enough the importance of strong foot controls. One of my guys placed a weak weld here once, and it caused me to run one of my customer's bikes through two fences and into a house.

## Oil Tanks

I've seen many forms of custom oil tanks, but I like to keep mine simple. Traditionally, a custom Big Twin has had an oil tank with a provision for a battery. I don't like this type of tank for several reasons. First, I avoid batteries when I can. Batteries have to be the most common source of trouble with custom bikes (besides unskilled mechanics).

Sometimes a battery is a necessary evil, however. For the past several years, I have been relocating my batteries to beneath the transmission. I have been removing the bar that typically runs under the transmission and putting the battery there. I make a mounting tray from 1/4-inch-thick aluminum diamond-plate that bolts to the frame's cross-members forward and aft of the transmission. Relocating the battery this way has allowed me to experiment with oil tank shapes and designs.

When I built the PsychoBilly Cadillac, I wanted to use Peterbilt truck emblems as the end panels of the tank. I built the tank out of steel, and epoxied the Pete emblems to the chrome-plated tank.

I also fabricated steel cooling fins, mostly for effect, and welded them to the top of the oil tank. I realized quickly that the fins were actually very functional. While sitting in Sturgis Main Street traffic, I reached down to touch the fins. They were scorching hot, which means they were drawing heat from the returned engine oil.

The Pete tank was a bit small, by virtue of the size of the emblems. It barely held 3 quarts. I have since created my Sneaky oil tanks, which hold 4 quarts and have bigger and more numerous fins. I put the first one in my ShitOuttaLuck bike and now use them in all of my customs. The nice thing about the Sneaky tanks is that they look very radical and race-influenced. They hold plenty of oil, which is necessary to cool a large-displacement Big Twin engine. Big Twins are air- and oil-cooled, and that hot chrome oil tank under the seat needs to be doing more than just holding oil until the pump sucks it through the engine.

I like to mount my oil tanks with the front hanging lower than the rear of the tank. It is a great look, but it also exposes the finned top area of the tank to oncoming cool air. The Sneaky tanks have internally plumbed vent and return tubes so that all of the oil lines are connected to the bottom of the tank.

As with my exhaust pipes, the oil tank needs to be mounted solidly in the bike. I always make two mounts on the top of the tank at the rear, and at least one mount on the bottom of the tank at the front. Cracked oil tanks mean slippery oil all over the back tire, which can be deadly.

All of my oil tanks have 1/8-inch NPT threaded fittings. I like the simplicity of using a standardized size of fitting, because it makes servicing the bike easier. I use 3/8-inch-diameter nippled slip-on fittings on the oil tank and engine. Between the fittings I use copper plumbing tubing from Ace Hardware. The tubing is easy to bend, cut, and manipulate. I cut it with a tubing cutter, and bend it with my hands. I use

2-inch-long sections of black rubber fuel line to connect the copper lines to the fittings at the pump, filter, and engine. I prefer to use factory-type oil line clamps. They do the job and look great.

Since I like vintage stuff, I used to always use early style canister oil filters. Riding to an event in North Carolina last year, the center stud that holds my early filter together broke while I was riding. I didn't know it until it was too late. My oil pump sent every drop of oil from my oil tank and engine to the filter, which was gone, and out onto the highway behind me. Panheads don't run far at 80 miles per hour with no oil, and I lunched mine that afternoon. Another thing that happened that afternoon was that I made a promise to myself to never run a canister type filter again. Now I mount mine Indian Larry style, toward the rear of the bike off the frame.

Ken and I discuss the mounting of my new oil tank. I like to run them with the front of the tank mounted much lower than the rear.

Ken mounts the oil tank at the rear using two steel slugs from the Choppers, Inc. Builder's Kit. A third slug will mount it near the front of the tank at the seat post.

I hold the tank in place as Ken tack welds the mounts to the frame and the oil tank.

## Seats

It is obvious: I like frame seats. Every bike I have ever built has a frame seat, except a couple that have Paul Cox air bags. Those ride pretty nice. I have always said a seat can make or break a bike. Good custom builders know this.

I like a small, thin seat that fits the shape of the frame. I like the edge of the seat to ride the centerline of the frame rails. My seats don't look comfortable, but they are. The key to comfort is not so much a function of cushion, but of posture. A good seat will cradle the rider's hips, support his lower back, and make him feel solid on the bike. If you feel like you are going to slide off the back fender when you twist the throttle, something isn't right.

The baseball-glove style that Paul Cox has made so popular is my favorite. Indian Larry always had them on his bikes, which is where I first saw that style years ago. It is hard to walk by a bike with a Danny Gray seat on it and not look, though. Danny's style is more elegant, where Paul's style is very raw. Passenger seats are necessary, but I keep mine small. I usually drill five holes in the pan before I have it upholstered. I place suction cups in the holes to keep the seat secured to the fender. A smaller seat ensures that Baby will be holding on tight. Make them work for it.

We make all of our seat pans out of aluminum or steel sheet metal. Ken draws out a paper template for the shape of the seat pan.

Eric and Ken with the outline for the seat pan transferred to the aluminum sheet metal.

Ken removes the excess metal from the seat pan's sheet with my PEXTO jump shear.

Eric finishes trimming the seat pan with the band saw.

Ken and Eric discuss the fitment of the seat pan to the frame and fender. Note that the seat pan is ready to be bent to match the template beneath it.

Eric holds the pan down to the frame as Ken bends the rear portion of the seat pan back.

Ken marks the seat pan for the holes he will drill for the locating pins that need to be welded to *Bobzilla*'s frame.

Eric TIG welds the seat locating pins to the frame. The pins are made from 1/4-inch-diameter round steel stock.

# CHAPTER SIX
## FINAL ASSEMBLY

Putting a bike together is relatively easy. Getting one down the highway safely is another story. Everyone is a hero until the inside of the pipes turn black. A few simple steps can help you out. I am notorious for riding the shit out of my bikes. I am going to share a few tips with you that allow me to do so.

The best advice I can give someone when starting a build is to be patient. It is a bad idea to start your build three days before Bike Week. You don't want a quick hair-cut, a quick tattoo, or a quick bike build. Trust me. In fact, my best bikes have been ones that I rode prior to painting and plating. It is much easier to fix a mistake or an over-sight when the bike is raw. Most builders don't do this, however, so I am going to proceed as if you won't either.

The first thing I do when my parts come back from the finishers is to prepare them for assembly. I always lay out all of the painted, polished, plated, powder-coated, and engraved parts to inspect them for quality. Parts can get shot off a polishing wheel and be permanently damaged and unusable. It is best to find that out before I am a week into final assembly or up against a deadline.

I also like to check to make sure everything I sent out has returned. I don't just bolt aftermarket parts to my bikes.

Most everything is handmade, so a missing part means hours of replacement time.

The frame is the best place to begin preparation. It is extremely important that any surface on the frame that will contact a metal component of the bike be devoid of any kind of coating. Coatings such as paint, powder coating, or chrome have an inherent thickness that was not present during the fabrication period. The added thickness they introduce will cause major problems that need to be elimi-nated now. Using a small, pneumatic angle grinder with a 120-grit sanding disc, I sand the coatings from these areas until the bare steel appears. It takes a light touch and a steady hand not to overdo it.

I typically use the threaded bungs from one of my Builder's Kits as frame mounts, as described in earlier chap-ters. Each threaded hole on the frame is cleaned with a threading tap and the debris in the threads is blown clear with compressed air. I also check that any bolt that will fit into a counterbore will still fit. If the counterbore has acquired buildup, I ream it out with a handheld ream. I also clean the machined surfaces on the frame where some of the critical components mount, such as the engine mounting pads, transmission mounts, foot control mounts,

*Bobzilla's* engine is a 1945 Knucklehead with a Linkert carburetor. I make the carb cover by cutting a steel flange with the plasma cutter and welding a piece of curved exhaust pipe to the flange.

fork neck cup surfaces, and the inner axle plates. Taking several hours to perform these operations is worthwhile in the end.

While the frame is devoid of its components. I run the wires and brake lines through the frame. I always wire my bikes as simply as possible, with the main junction of all the wiring being at the key switch under the seat. Almost exclusively, I mount the key switch in this location.

Two 14-gauge wires run through the frame's backbone and exit near the neck. One is for the headlight low beam, the other is for the high beam. Two 16-gauge wires run through the frame's lower rear left leg behind the engine and exit through the license tag bracket. One will power the rear running light, and the other will actuate the brake light. These wires will connect to the brake light banjo-bolt switch, which will be located at the high pressure fitting on the rear brake master cylinder, located at the right-hand-side foot control.

The 14-gauge power feed to these two wires will run down through the seat post, exit at its base, and make its connection at the running light side of the brake switch. I also wire the 14-gauge power feed to the ignition coil(s) through the seat post. The most important wire sharing the inside of the seat post is the 12-gauge main power feed, which runs between the output terminal from the voltage rectifier/regulator to the "Batt," or long post of the 30-amp circuit breaker that I mount conveniently within inches of the key switch under the seat. This wire transports the electric current from the supply source to the rest of the machine.

The short post on the 30-amp circuit breaker is connected to the "Batt" terminal on the key switch with a short 12-gauge wire. If a battery is being used in the bike, a 12-gauge wire should run from the battery positive (+) terminal to the "Batt," or long post of the 30-amp circuit breaker. The circuit breaker isolates the expensive and delicate battery and charging components from the remainder of the bike's wiring and circuitry. In the event of an electrical short, the circuit breaker opens the connection between its two posts, ensuring that no damage will occur to the charging components.

Also mounted under the seat in close proximity to the key switch is the Hi-Lo beam switch. It has three terminals. The center "hot" terminal should be connected to the "Acc" terminal on the key switch with a 14-gauge wire.

The side view of the intake shows how the curvature of the pipe allows me to clear the exhaust.

I am using an old car emblem as a carb cover. In order to mount it, I drill and cut a piece of flat steel stock to which I will bolt the emblem.

I bend the flat steel in the vise with a small sledge.

The steel mounting strap bolted to the car emblem. The bends will space the emblem away from the intake pipe, allowing adequate airflow into the carburetor.

I hold the cover in place and check the way it looks. I plan to mount the emblem at this angle over the pipes.

I will TIG weld the steel strap to the pipe as shown here. Note the air space around the strap.

I first tack weld the strap into place, then bolt the cover to it to see if it is where it needs to be.

The finished carb cover looks great. It is a die-cast piece from the 1940s or 1950s. It was cheap and easy to make. And it is cool.

I make the clutch release linkage for the suicide shift from a length of 3/8-inch-diameter steel round stock. I cut the stock to length and bevel the edges with a grinder to prep for welding.

Most guys thread the end of the link rod using a threading die. I prefer to weld a threaded bolt to the end of the link rod. This saves time, and makes it easy to change the length of the rod if needed.

I make the shift arm from a 14-inch-long section of 1-inch diameter aluminum round stock. One end will be threaded to attach the arm to the shifter, and the other is threaded for the shift knob. I center each end to prep for drilling.

The drilling operation is performed in my lathe.

The taper I cut is visible in this shot. After I make my final pass with the cutting tool, I sand the arm with a strip of emery cloth to smooth out its finish.

I plan to taper-cut the shift arm, so I move the lathe's tailstock in to support the free end.

I am going to ball-mill the shifter arm—that is, I drill shallow ornamental holes in its surface—so I have to fixture it in my Bridgeport milling machine. I am using a rotary table with a lathe chuck welded to it to rotate the part. Here I fixture the part with the rotary table and tailstock.

The rotary table allows me to add ball-milled dimples evenly around the shifter arm.

This shot shows the staggered ball-milling operation. Note the black concentric marks I made around the shifter arm with a Sharpie. These marks are simply visual indicators, so I know where to drop the cutting tool.

Here is the finished shifter arm. It still needs to be polished, but all of the machining is done.

I'm using an evil Tiki head that my friend Steve Lanier gave me as a gift a while ago. He made this thing himself, and I think it will work perfectly with the rest of the bike.

We make our own foot controls at Choppers, Inc. I prefer to run a Performance-Machine 5/8-inch-bore master cylinder, mounted backward. The pedal pivots from the same axis that the foot peg is mounted on. These foot controls are light, sturdy, and minimalist.

# INDEX

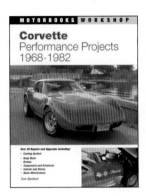

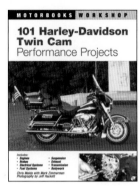
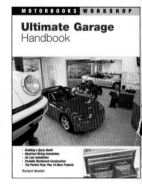